Praise for

50 Ways to Worry Less Now

"*50 Ways to Worry Less Now* reads like a compendium of the world's wisdom on successful living. One can open practically any page and find concrete ideas to live positively in the present. These are no set of abstractions found in self-help books; rather they are lessons Langer has learned from painful experience. She is candid and vulnerable in this book that is worth keeping close at hand. Many will find connections to their own struggles now and in the past. I am buying copies for my grandchildren."

—**Dr. Bob Garmston**, Emeritus Professor,
California State University

"Gigi Langer has written a great book. Because I have been in recovery for more than four decades, and have written a few books myself, I wasn't actually expecting to get a lot of 'new information.' Nor was I expecting to adopt some of her tools for successfully dealing with some of the niggling problems I was born to experience. I was wrong on both counts. It has been a long time since I read a self-help book that inspired me to take notes. I'm quite certain that anyone who chooses to read this book will find, as I did, a host of very helpful suggestions that will not only change his or her life, but the lives of everyone encountered."

—**Karen Casey**, best-selling author of *Each Day
a New Beginning*, *Daily Meditations for Practicing
the Course*, and *Keepers of the Wisdom*.

"Gigi has written a jewel of a book with sharp insight, an open honest heart, timeless wisdom, and inspiration galore. A healing masterpiece if one chooses to use the tools."

—**LiRa Bennett**, President, A Place of Well-Being, Inc.

"This book is a gift to those of us who yearn to defeat worry, negativity, and self-doubt. It is beautifully written, clearly organized, and filled with life-changing wisdom. Gigi has truly led the way to successful living and made it possible for us to follow."

—**Ginny Chism**

"*50 Ways to Worry Less Now: Reject Negative Thinking to Find Peace, Clarity, and Connection* comes from an author who is personally as well as professionally familiar with her topic. Thirty years ago, she used alcohol and professional obligations to escape worries. It took a blend of recovery programs, therapies, and spiritual insights to finally lead her to calm her own fears and those of others; and this book reflects this process, synthesizing it into four life strategies and some fifty tools that squelch negative thinking patterns.

"Plenty of books advocate countering negative thinking; but too few actually provide step-by-step measures on how to do so. Others simply choose a singular path and follow it. The pleasure of this book lies in its examples, specific exercises, and injections of how the author used various routines to find her way out of negativity. The result is an important set of guidelines that any reader can easily follow, highly recommended for anyone who worries too much, lives too hard a life, and searches for a better way."

—**D. Donovan**, Senior Reviewer, Midwest Book Review

"A veritable treasure map of strategies for the reader whose life or relationships have been diminished by worrying. Gigi Langer is both a field guide and fellow traveler who has skillfully navigated the difficult terrain using an array of clinical, medical, and philosophical sources. One of the best 'How To' manuals I've read."

—**Coleen Travers**, LCSW

ACKNOWLEDGMENTS

A very special thank you goes to my husband, Peter, my rock and greatest champion. I couldn't have done it without your patience and love . . . and all those snacks served to me as I was typing away!

I offer deep gratitude to my circle of friends who support my growth and dreams: Sue Ahrenhold, Liz Audette, Gloria Brooks, Lorilyn Bryan, Dawn Champanois, Amy Colton, Anna Devlin, Sue DuPree, Cathy Freeman, Eileen Grady, Virginia Harlow, Maureen Harrington, Mary Cay Johns, Bethann Jorgenson, Andrea Lanning, Deirdre Limoges, Marianne Martus, Susan Morales, Paula Phaneuf, Kathleen Riley, Amy Thomas, and Coleen Travers.

I also thank the many readers of this manuscript for their encouragement and wise suggestions: Alexandra Dixon, Marcie Foster, Pam Gerber, Kathy Harenda, Nancy Harknett, Ginna Jordan, Sharon Kalbfleisch, Bob Kraft, Ward Larson, Sheena Luther, Christine McCully, Annabelle Nesbit, Paula Phaneuf, Jamie Schooley, Rosalie Skinner, Bernadette Thibodeau, Nancy Trecha, Cissy Webb, and Janice Weber. Special thanks to Ginger Wakem for her many hours of editing and enthusiastic support of all aspects of this project.

My chief editor, Anita LeBlanc, and earlier editors, Betsy Kirchen and Nina Amir, made the book readable and concise without losing any of the "juice." Special thanks to Sandy Dorda for her inspired photography and to the gracious cover designer, Kelly Zorn. Maria McGowan, my social media marketing coach, has saved me from chronic "digital distress."

The genius, witty typographer, Tom Halley, and patient, expert proof-reader, Betsy Dietrich, held my hand through the final stages of publishing. Thank you, team, for creating a beautiful and accessible book!

Finally, I'm grateful to my family for permitting me to share our stories: my mother, Cece Wakem Mohlman, an avid reader and connoisseur of language; my father, the earthy, charming, and eccentric Ted Mohlman; and my sisters and brother.

In memory of Jane Stallings, my spiritual mother and mentor; and Babette Cain, a friend in recovery.

50 Ways to Worry Less Now

Reject Negative Thinking
to Find Peace, Clarity, and Connection

Gigi Langer, PhD

Possum Hill Press, 2720 Calloway Ct., Canton, MI 48188

Typographer: Tom Halley, Tom Halley Typography. *Th.T@mindspring.com*
Editor: Anita LeBlanc, The Write Word. *thewriteword@sbcglobal.net*
Proofreader: Betsy Dietrich, *Betsykmd@att.net*
Cover Design: Kelly Zorn, Z Design Studio. *kellyzorn@me.com*
Cover Photo: Sandy Dorda. *lemonlanefreshrestyled@gmail.com*

Permissions have been acquired from the following to use their material:
Byron Katie, *Loving What Is*. New York: Three Rivers Press, 2003.
Iris DeMent, (song). "No Time To Cry." Album: *My Life*, Warner Brothers, 1994.
Colin Tipping, *Radical Forgiveness*. Louisville, CO: Sounds True, 2010.
Coleman Barks, translator of Rumi's poem, "The Guest House."

First printing 2018
18 17 16 15 14 13 12   7 6 5 4 3 2 1

Manufactured in the United States of America

Cataloging-in-Publication Data is available from the Library of Congress.
ISBN: 978-0-9991220-0-6 (cloth. : alk. paper)
ISBN: 978-0-9991220-1-3 (ePub)
ISBN: 978-0-9991220-2-0 (Mobipocket)
ISBN: 978-0-9991220-3-7 (ePDF)

To order, or to learn more, please visit the author's website at *www.gigilanger.com*.
Facebook, Gigi Langer Author; Twitter, @gigi_langer

TABLE OF CONTENTS

PREFACE

If you want your life to be a magnificent story, then begin
by realizing that you are the author and every day you have
the opportunity to write a new page.

—Mark Houlahan

Does your mind automatically tune into the worry-and-fear channel? Are you suffering from worry about relationship difficulties, family issues, excessive eating, overworking, ongoing pain, illness, financial woes, addictions, or damaging anger? Do you want to escape your stressful thoughts about the future or regrets from the past? Are you seeking freedom from depression, a general sense of discontent, or a feeling of low self-worth? Up until now, you may have been trying to change these damaging patterns with the same old frustrating results.

The good news is: *You don't have to be a prisoner of your worries, no matter what's going on in your life.* Here you'll learn how to use Four Strategies and fifty tools to gain:

- *Peace.* Manage your life challenges with wisdom, hope, and gratitude—no matter what is going on.
- *Clarity.* Discover your true self to fulfill your greatest dreams without limitations.
- *Connection.* Create relationships that blossom and thrive, while serving others in loving ways.

What's pleasantly surprising is that you don't need to use the Four Strategies or any of the other tools perfectly. You merely need to exert a consistent, honest attempt to apply the ones that appeal to you.

A lifelong struggle with my own worries prompted my search for solutions that work. This book shares what I've learned from my training in psychology, as well as over thirty years applying tools from recovery programs, cognitive therapy, energy work, scientific literature, and a variety of spiritual teachings.

Of course, if you are troubled by a situation that poses a threat to your well-being, you should take assertive action to secure your own safety. Further, if you are a survivor of abuse or trauma, or if you are having thoughts of harming yourself, I strongly encourage you to seek help from a licensed therapist, hospital, or mental health clinic. Those of you currently in therapy or a support group will find this book a helpful enhancement to your work.

Will It Work?

Backed by a variety of research studies, my own experience, and work with others, I can tell you with confidence the Four Strategies and other tools will free you from the tyranny of worry and fear. Here are some of the challenges I've faced and overcome.

- *Relationship failures.* I divorced my third husband when I was thirty-nine years old, convinced I could never be happily married. Three years later, I married the man of my dreams. We recently celebrated our twenty-eighth anniversary.
- *Chronic pain.* I struggled with back pain for fifteen years. Then both of my shoulders "froze" for two merciless years. After surgery and physical therapy, I am now free of pain and in excellent health.
- *Dysfunctional family.* I suffered from many of the characteristics found in children of alcoholic parents: anxiety, depression, and low self-esteem. Through years of work and support from others, I've been able to uncover and heal these characteristics.
- *Codependence.* When my dear friend battled cancer and, later, my husband resumed drinking alcohol, I discovered my

overreliance on others for my happiness. Over time, I found my own true source of security.

- *Overwork and perfectionism.* As a college professor, I wrestled with fierce professional jealousies and insecurities, along with a tendency toward overwork and perfectionism. Eventually, I learned how to be both productive *and* content in my work.
- *Abuse.* I discovered memories of early abuse, healed its wounds, and forgave those who had harmed me.
- *Alcohol dependence.* For many years, marijuana and alcohol were ruining my relationships and inhibiting my power. Now, I've been clean and sober for thirty-one years and have helped hundreds of women recover from alcohol and drug addiction.

Although my story includes these specific challenges, you can use the Four Strategies and the many tools to transform almost any difficult aspect of life that's troubling you: illness, concerns about loved ones, negativity, low self-esteem, depression, trauma, or anxiety.

"I've Done This Too Many Times"

By the time I was thirty-six, I lived in a self-created jail of fear and worry. I had a new doctorate from Stanford University and a college teaching position in Michigan. Yet I was more miserable than I'd ever been in my life.

One afternoon, I took a walk to my favorite tavern and chose a seat at the bar. As I sat contemplating my face through the bottles lined along the mirror, I thought, "How could I have gotten to this place again? I've done this too many times."

Shafts of sunlight pierced the blinds the same way they had at my regular bar at Stanford. Eventually, a couple of guys in business suits came in and sat near me. I thought one of them was rather attractive, so I struck up a conversation. During the next hour, we chatted and had a few more drinks.

It didn't matter that my third husband was at home waiting for me. I didn't care that I would be driving home in a drunken stupor. I only knew I would stay there until the beer, sex, and drugs took the pain away.

After small talk escalated into flirtation, I called home and fed my husband a story about being out with some of my students. A few hours later, I called and said that I wouldn't be home until quite late. Then I left with the guy I'd picked up. We went to buy cocaine, and then drove to his home and had sex. Only through good fortune did I make it home safely at 2:00 a.m. I told my husband more lies the next morning to cover up my misadventures.

Disgusted by my behavior, I decided I needed help and went to see a therapist. After a few sessions, I found his approach wasn't helping me. I did, however, receive one gift when I asked his secretary to suggest a new route to my office. Following her directions, I drove along a winding oak-bowered road and approached a placid river. Suddenly, something deep inside me said, "I'd love to live near a place just like this."

Now, many years later, and after considerable work on my own fears and worries, I find myself living in an old farmhouse along the same tree-lined road overlooking the river. My husband and I have a happy marriage, I'm at peace, and I can honestly say I love my life.

What Happened?

How did I change from that miserable woman staring at bottles in a bar to the contented person I am now? While my transformation has been deceptively simple, it hasn't been easy. The secret? I've learned to overcome the negative thoughts causing my most devastating worries and fears.

I call such thoughts *whispered lies*. Sitting in that bar, my mind whispered to me, "You blew it again," "You're a bad person," and "If only your husband would change, you could be happy." These lies were clogging my life with blame, guilt, and resentment. Further, they were keeping me from discovering and expressing my best self.

If you want to overcome your own whispered lies, fears, and worries, read on. You'll find the Four Strategies and wide variety of techniques key to your success. I hope you'll find yourself identifying with my stories, and those of others, about our challenges and victories.

Guided exercises throughout the book will help you apply the tools to your own situations. You may want to use a special computer file, journal, or binder for the exercises and other notes you wish to keep. Tool 5 in chapter 2 explains various options for journal entries. For easy reference, Appendix B lists the Four Strategies and all fifty tools.

So, let's get started! I created this quiz to help you determine your own worry quotient.

Time for Action!
What's Your Worry Quotient?

Freedom from worry brings you a host of benefits. According to Dr. Amit Sood's *Mayo Clinic Guide to Stress-Free Living*, people who worry less have better physical health, lower risks of stroke or heart disease, and higher overall survival rates. They also have better emotional health, less depression, more harmonious relationships, and are more equipped to solve life's problems. Read each statement, decide if it's true for you, record the corresponding number of points, and add up your score.

Thoughts and Habits   **Score**

1. When I tune into what I'm thinking, I am usually:
    a) Remembering something about the past (+1)
    b) Pondering something in the future (+1)
    c) Focusing on what is going on right now (0)
2. I often find myself wishing things were different. (+1)
3. I wish I could take better care of my own needs (e.g., exercise, rest, nutrition, social support). (+1)
4. When I'm struggling with a situation in my life, I tell the story about it over and over. (+1)
5. I often clench my teeth or feel tension in my shoulders, stomach, or neck. (+1)
6. I meditate or sit still regularly. (0)

7. I wish I could worry less about:
   a) My own health (+1)
   b) My loved ones (+1)
   c) The opinions of others about me (+1)
   d) My finances (+1)
   e) World events (+1)
   f) My past mistakes (+1)
8. I often stop to savor my surroundings (music, a pet, nature, etc.). (0)
9. I am hesitating to pursue a dream I've had for a while. (+1)
10. I often put others' needs ahead of my own. (+1)

Total Number of Points: Your Worry Quotient
- Score 11–14: I need to find a way to attain peace of mind and happiness.
- Score 7–10: I could use some new techniques to help me worry less.
- Score 0–6: I probably have strategies that already work well for me (or I might be in denial).

Don't worry if your score seems high. According to the National Institute of Mental Health's website, almost one in five Americans struggle with worry and non-severe anxiety.

My Hope for You

My sincerest wish is that you will overcome your own worries so you can be happy, relaxed, and fulfill your dreams; that, even during your troubling times, you will find peace, wisdom, and appropriate actions. Finally, I hope your victories will inspire others to reject their own whispered lies and negative thinking.

I encourage you to try the tools in this book that appeal to you and take note of the ones you might use in the future. I would love to hear how you're overcoming your own worries and challenges. Please contact me with any questions you might have through Facebook, Gigi Langer Author, or my website, *www.gigilanger.com*.

Chapter 1

Four Powerful Strategies to Overcome Worry

*Worry can light on our shoulders or sink its teeth into our
flesh. Worry can become such a habit that it may actually take
over most of our waking and dreaming hours.*

—Chinese proverb

Do you have a voice in your head that says, "If I can't get (*fill in the
blank*) to happen, I'll never be happy," or "If (*fill in the blank*) happens,
I'll never get over it?" If so, you're not alone. I call such messages *whispered lies* because they sabotage our dreams and desires. And they simply are not true.

When life isn't working, it's usually because we're trying to force things
to go our way. Unfortunately, we don't have as much control over external events as we might imagine, and worrying about them just makes us
feel worse. You might be able to relate to the following example.

You're on your way to an important appointment with your doctor
and you've left the house just a little late. You find yourself waiting in
a long line of cars with left-turn signals blinking. When the cars finally
begin to inch forward, you realize you might not make it through the
light. You look at your watch, clench your jaw, and think, "I can't miss
this appointment." Your stomach begins to churn as you imagine having
to wait several more weeks to see the doctor. Suddenly, a big black car
cuts in front of you. He's the last one to make it through the light. You
bang your hands on the steering wheel and yell, "Who in the hell does he

think he is?" Then your mind whispers, "I'll never get in to see the doctor! My symptoms will get worse and I'll suffer even more. Why does this always happen to me?"

I'll bet you've had a similar experience. I sure have. It's hard to keep such incidents from prompting a hissy fit, often with dire results. For instance, we might drive recklessly in the traffic or speak rudely to the doctor's receptionist. When we arrive home, we could hurt a loved one with critical or impatient words, followed by more upsetting thoughts—for example, "People just don't understand me!"

You're probably thinking your problems are much bigger than a traffic jam. Of course they are. That's why you picked up this book. Perhaps you're struggling with a divorce, breakup, illness, bankruptcy, or a loved one's addiction. Possibly, you're living in your own personal hell where you find yourself dreading the future or replaying painful scenes from the past. You'll find the Four Strategies I present here can overcome even the most serious worries because most of them are based on lies.

Those Pesky Whispered Lies

I define whispered lies as the negative mental or emotional messages that cause distress. My friends say they come from the not-so-helpful "committee in my head". For instance, the belief "If I want to be liked, I must look good" produces worries about one's appearance and behavior. A few more examples include:

- "I'll never have enough money."
- "I always sabotage my success."
- "Relationships just don't work for me."
- "We could all be happy if only Dad would stop drinking."

Although many of our whispered lies concern ourselves, they often focus on our children, spouses, friends, or relatives—for instance, the last example about the father's drinking. Other distressing beliefs involve institutions, as in "If the government would just change this policy, we'd all be better off."

Even though it might be true that Dad ought to stop drinking or the government should make changes, *these events have no control over your own happiness.* You can find peace of mind under any circumstances because *you're in charge of what you think about.*

Where do our false beliefs come from? We formed many of them during our childhoods as we sought ways to feel safe and loved. For instance, children who receive attention only when they get a high grade or win competitions often believe "I must perform well to be loved." Other whispered lies, for example, "I'm a loser," are the result of the unkind words or actions of insensitive people, perhaps relatives, teachers, siblings, or lovers.

Most of our worries are fueled by false stories installed into our minds long ago, just waiting for opportunities to be confirmed. Wayne Dyer wrote in *Wishes Fulfilled: Mastering the Art of Manifesting* that everything our brain "knows" is based on past experiences. Because of this, when an event resembles—even in a small way—an old painful one, our mind interprets the new event according to a long-standing negative belief. Since most whispered lies live largely in our unconscious, we're often unaware of them.

To illustrate the power of negative thinking, consider why I failed at romantic love so many times during my twenties and thirties. I wanted to believe that love was possible for me, but my past had taught me the lie "I'm not worthy of love." This belief lived so strongly in my mind that, even when a man loved me deeply, I couldn't believe it was true. After several months, I would become convinced that he wasn't fulfilling my needs. These worries made me so demanding that I soon snuffed out all the happiness and joy of new love. When it ended, I'd tell myself, "I just don't deserve love!" Until I got honest and started healing my faulty thinking, I had no hope of enjoying a happy relationship.

Reject Worry's Lies to Find Peace

In this book, you'll learn how to counteract your worries by applying the Four Strategies in figure 1.1. These powerful tactics dissolve the negative beliefs (whispered lies) underlying your fears. As you use this system, I strongly suggest that you meet with healthy friends or a therapist to share your concerns, as well as your progress. Guidelines for choosing these people appear at the end of this chapter.

Get Honest	Admit that your worries have kept you stuck in unhappiness.
Claim Power	Claim a source of positive power to overcome your worries through your mind, spirit, or body energy.
Make Choices	Choose a new future and commit to do the necessary work to achieve it.
Use Growth Practices	Consistently use a variety of tools to dissolve your worries. As you gain a peaceful perspective, you will act with wisdom, heal past wounds, repair relationships, and find true happiness.

Figure 1.1 Four Strategies to Overcome Worry

Here's how the Four Strategies might look when applied to the afore-mentioned traffic situation. First, the driver *honestly* admits how upset she is, and tunes into the tension in her jaw and belly. She then notices, without judgment, her whispered lies—for example, "I just thought 'That guy is a real jerk!' and I've convinced myself I'll never make it to my appointment."

She follows that realization with "If I can stop worrying, I can access the *power* of clarity." She then makes the *choice* to cease upsetting her-self. She might seek a different perspective by thinking, "I have no con-trol over this traffic. This would be frustrating for anyone. I'm willing to trust that I'll get to the doctor at just the right time."

As she moves her focus away from her irritation and fear, she *prac-tices* directing it toward constructive thoughts and feelings. She begins with the tool of deep breathing. In her calmer state, she tries to feel com-passion toward the driver who cut her off. Perhaps he's had a bad day or family emergency. Finally, she uses visualization to imagine the office receptionist being helpful and kind. As her negative thinking continues to make a bid for her attention, she persists in using these tools.

In a short time, the next right action occurs to her. She thinks, "I'm going to call the receptionist and ask if I can keep my appointment if I'm thirty minutes late." When her call is put on hold, she breathes calmly. Soon, she learns that the doctor is behind schedule and being late for the appointment is no problem. She relaxes and enjoys the ride.

I can imagine you're thinking that the driver should have been more assertive, perhaps by immediately seeking a detour. Here's an important point: *Using these strategies does* not *mean that you never take strong action.* They simply allow you to delay acting until you've gained a little wisdom. As a result of your new perspective, if you *are* meant to do something, you'll have the direction you need.

Free Up Your Life Force

Imagine your life as an open channel. When your worries and whispered lies clog the channel, only a tiny bit of wisdom, peace, or happiness can flow through it. You dissolve these barriers as you look honestly at your whispered lies, claim the power to alter them, and then choose new ways of thinking and living. Your consistent use of growth practices and tools will keep your channel open, so loving care comes into your life and goes out toward others.

Meditation is one of the simplest ways to experience peace and goodness flowing through the channel of your being. Although there are many beneficial forms of meditation, one of my favorites involves mindfully focusing on your breathing. This practice works because it leaves no room for negative thoughts to enter the mind.

Time for Action!
Tool 1. Mindfulness Meditation

Meditation is a powerful antidote to worry, anxiety, depression, chronic pain, and substance abuse. As reported by Holzel, Carmody, and Vangel in *Psychiatry Research: Neuroimaging*, mindfulness meditation shrinks the parts of the brain responsible for fear and stress. It is no wonder so many of those who meditate stay calm and find positive solutions in the face of trouble. To try it, seek a quiet spot where you won't be disturbed, and set a timer for two minutes.

1. Sit with your back straight. If you're more comfortable lying down, do so, perhaps with your knees bent or a pillow under them. Place your hands in a comfortable position. Close your eyes. Relax your jaw, mouth, and tongue.
2. Now simply notice one breath at a time. Focus on where you most feel the breath. Is it in your nostrils, your belly, the expansion of your rib cage, or somewhere else?
3. Imagine each in-breath draws in a positive force that dissolves your whispered lies. Imagine each out-breath enlarges the space for wisdom, peace, and joy to enter your mind.
4. Refrain from evaluating or judging yourself. When you notice that you're distracted, simply acknowledge the fact and switch your attention back to the sensations of breathing.
5. Don't worry if you spend a lot of time lost in your thoughts. Every time you redirect your attention back to your breath, you increase your ability to dissolve your worries.
6. After two minutes, stop the practice and take a moment to absorb its effects.

If you realize that you couldn't stop thinking, that's fine. The point is to merely let your thoughts drop into the background as you focus your attention on your breathing. It takes practice, but it's worth it.

Try mindfulness meditation for two or more minutes every day for a week. You'll likely find your troubles seem less dramatic than they appeared before. If this isn't right the tool for you, many more follow.

Saved by the Four Strategies

One night, my friend Mary called and asked for my advice. She had just met the affluent mother of one of her daughter's friends. When the woman asked Mary where she lived, Mary didn't want to say she resided in a small apartment with her three children. Instead, she gave a vague answer. After this encounter, she began to feel very uncomfortable.

Mary began our conversation by *honestly* describing the situation and her embarrassment. Together we identified her whispered lies: "I'm a loser," and "People will only like me if I match their standard of living." She also admitted that her need to look good in the eyes of others was a long-standing problem.

Mary felt powerless over her negative thinking and past efforts to correct it. By talking with me, a trusted friend, she began to claim the *power and courage* to overcome her fears. As we talked together over the next few weeks, I encouraged Mary to *choose* a vision for her future life and to use the following *growth practices* to overcome her whispered lies.

- *Positive affirmation (tool 16 in chapter 4)*. I asked Mary to write a statement of what she most wanted in her life as if it had already happened. She wrote: "I have freedom from my self-punishing thoughts and economic security for my family." She followed my suggestion to read the statement aloud as often as possible, visualize it as if it were already done, and feel gratitude for the results.
- *The Golden Key (tool 23 in chapter 5)*. I told Mary to notice every time she was worrying, and then to shift her thoughts toward any connection she felt with positive power. Because she had a religious affiliation, she chose to focus on God. (Chapter 3 provides a variety of other ways to think about a source of loving power.)
- *Gratitude list (tool 15 in chapter 3)*. I recommended that Mary write a daily list of five things she was grateful for, without repeating any of them for an entire week.

My conversations with Mary began in January. During the next few months, she met with me, connected with her positive power, affirmed her life choices, and used the suggested tools. She even added some new ones; for example, she increased her participation in a support group.

In March, Mary experienced what she described as "a miracle." She was freed from her self-judgment and found peace with her current living situation. A month later, Mary was offered a lease on a gorgeous three-bedroom home for very low rent. Then, just as I was revising this chapter, she called to say she had received a promotion at work with a big pay raise.

Notice that Mary's changes did not come all at once. She followed the process with patience and determination. Another of her crucial actions was joining with others and me.

When we're in the grip of our worries, seeking help is the last thing that occurs to many of us. By connecting with others, however, we can explore questions such as, "How might I see this differently?" "What do I want as an outcome?" or "What growth tools might help me?"

The next section will help you find the right people to share your worries and growth.

We Can't Do It Alone

Talking things over with healthy friends will help you immensely when you're in the thrall of your own worries. The following quote from Karen Casey's book, *Worthy of Love,* perfectly expresses the importance of *growth partners*: "We contribute to each other's search for understanding, and the spiritual quest that's at our center finds its resting place in one another's hearts."

It can be challenging to find healthy friends. I understand this because I was a loner before I began to address my negative thinking. If you have difficulty finding growth partners, I encourage you to be open-minded and to keep searching. Even one person with whom you can share your work with the Four Strategies is enough for now.

Connecting with growth-minded people helps you for at least three reasons. First, it's easier to be honest with yourself when you're around people who openly share their personal struggles and victories. As you listen to them, you can tune into your own feelings and uncover some of your own whispered lies.

Second, with such friends, you can find the self-acceptance and hope that may elude you when you're alone with your worries. As others describe how they've handled similar troubles, you begin to realize you're not the only one who has felt this way, and you too can discover a way to deal with your challenges.

Third, you'll often find power and guidance through others. As people tell their own stories, you might hear just the words you need. In turn, you may hear yourself saying things that are helpful not only to your friends, but also to yourself.

If all of this is true, then why do so many people resist joining with others for support? The culprit may be one or more of the following whispered lies: "I'm all alone in the world," or "I can figure this out all by myself." Most people never question such beliefs until they lose a loved one, get sick, fired, divorced, or experience some other tragedy. In such cases, the support of healthy friends or a therapist is often essential.

Alone No More

The story of my friend, Sue, illustrates how one person went from being a loner to discovering the importance of connecting with others. From grade three on, Sue had been shuffled from foster home to foster home. As a result, she suffered from a devastating pair of false beliefs: "I must be fiercely independent to survive," and "I'm not worthy of anyone's care."

By the time she was in her mid-forties, those lies kept her isolated at home with her three cats and a bottle of booze. When Sue first came to our group's meetings, she rarely spoke. When some of us told her, "Let us love you until you can love yourself," she didn't believe it. We had to convince her.

Despite her relapses, jail time, and financial troubles, we continued to support her. Over time, Sue honestly admitted her problem, found a source of positive power, chose to heal her life, and practiced many of the techniques in this book. After several months of sobriety, she began to join us for outings, sharing her generous heart and sense of humor.

One day, a truck hit Sue's motorcycle and broke her back, keeping her at home for months with a cast around her torso. Our growth group pitched in to take care of her. A year later, Sue stood in front of us, her eyes brimming with tears, as she thanked all the women who had helped her. She finally awoke to the fact that she was not alone.

Who's a Good Growth Partner?

You might think, "I hate groups! I prefer talking to one person." In this case, consider a counselor or therapist as your first growth partner, but be picky. Give the person a few months to work with you, and make sure you're willing to move on to another professional if necessary. If cost is a challenge, many agencies, colleges, churches, and universities offer sliding-scale or free services.

If you choose to share your personal challenges with a friend, you'll need to distinguish between the helpful and the unhelpful ones. This first tip may surprise you: *Your best growth partners probably won't come from your family.* While your family members are certainly an important part of your life, they may unwittingly reinforce the very same patterns you're trying to overcome. Give yourself some time to heal before you share deeply with family members.

I also suggest you *choose an individual who holds no sexual attraction for you.* If you ignore this advice, your goals for personal growth may take a backseat to the romantic imperative, with damaging results.

Be sure to consider *how you feel after talking to the person.* If you feel more agitation than hope, try sharing your vulnerabilities with someone else. Here are a few ways to distinguish a helpful friend from a less helpful one.

- *"It's all about me," rather than "It's all about you."*
  - ✓ A less helpful friend responds by sharing her own troubles. If she can't switch her focus to your concerns, then she may not have the skills to support your well-being.
  - ✓ A helpful friend listens, carefully summarizes your thoughts and feelings, and asks questions to understand and support you. If this friend shares her own story, it's offered only to give you hope; then she returns the focus to you.

- *"Here's my solution," rather than "Here's how to access wise guidance."*
  - ✓ A less helpful friend suggests immediate solutions that attempt to control the situation. Because he is uneasy with your discomfort, his goal is to fix it right now. Such actions often make the situation worse rather than better.
  - ✓ A helpful friend offers ideas and tools that bring you peace and intuitive guidance. He'll remind you that a serene state of mind will lead you to the best actions.

- *"Let's focus on the problem," rather than "Let's find a place of peace."*
  - ✓ A less helpful friend wants to hear the lurid details. She commiserates about how terrible your situation is and helps you justify your pain. Such friends end up reinforcing your resentments, fears, and worries.
  - ✓ A helpful friend refuses to escalate your fears by "awfulizing" events. She might suggest that you accept the situation as it is for now, and work toward a peaceful state of mind. Finally, she reassures you that this situation will find resolution in the best way for all, and that it may take time.

What's a Helpful Group?

If you feel drawn to a group setting, it's easy to find like-minded people collectively seeking healthy solutions for life's challenges. Such groups gather in churches, synagogues, mosques, meditation centers, hospitals, and community organizations all over the world.

You might find growth-oriented people in yoga classes, book study groups, or other community events. Check out your local listings or ask your friends, doctor, or counselor for ideas. When I recently made the move to a new town, I found the app called Meetup to be a useful directory of gatherings for almost any topic under the sun.

When trying to overcome the fears and worries associated with your own—or a loved one's—alcoholism, substance abuse, overeating, mounting debt, or gambling, a group that follows the Twelve Steps of Alcoholics Anonymous (AA) is a good choice. If you don't want to go to AA, Celebrate Recovery uses a Christian approach to these and many other life problems. Other options include Refuge Recovery and SMART Recovery. Appendix C contains more information.

Most personal-growth experts suggest attending a group four or five times to determine if it's helpful. To select the right one, I suggest you settle down in a quiet spot and say aloud something like this, "I am finding the right group to benefit myself and others." Then go out and look for the following characteristics.

- *A welcoming and open atmosphere.* Find an inclusive group where you feel that your desire to grow and learn has value. Such gatherings are free of cliques; you don't want your group to feel like high school! And beware of those that pressure you to contribute large amounts of money or time.
- *Clarity of purpose and organization.* The most helpful groups have a clearly written statement of purpose and a set of guidelines. Notice whether these are announced and honored.
- *Confidentiality.* Anything said in the group should not be repeated elsewhere. A written or verbal statement of this agreement is highly recommended.
- *Honesty and openness.* Listen to the nature of the discussions. Are people taking risks by sharing their vulnerabilities? If so, this group has a high level of trust and honesty, two essential ingredients for your growth.
- *Lack of advice.* Beware of others' attempts to control you or give advice. As you listen to the members share, take what works for you and leave the rest behind.

Time for Action!
Tool 2. Finding Your Growth Partners

Going it alone rarely brings freedom from worry. Scientific studies show that people who enjoy loving, supportive friendships have better health, longevity, happiness, and resilience in the face of troubles—as reported by Brené Brown in her books *The Gifts of Imperfection* and *Daring Greatly*. Whom will you select to support your efforts to overcome your worries and whispered lies?

1. List two healthy friends or a therapist you're willing to meet.
2. Find the name, time, and location of one or two groups that might provide helpful support during a current life challenge.
3. In your journal, write your plans for finding growth partners.
4. Enter a reminder in your calendar and follow through on your plans.

You'll end up with the right friends or professionals to help you find freedom from your negative thinking. This is not a go-it-alone job!

Whether you're joining with an individual or a group, the Four Strategies begin with *honestly* looking at your fearful thinking and what it's costing you.

Time for Action!
Tool 3. Your Worries and Their Consequences

Here you'll identify your worries and imagine your life without their negative effects. Read the three examples below: The first is one of my own worries; the second and third examples concern other common situations. If you feel ready, follow the directions to complete the exercise.

1. Think about a situation that's troubling you. To get the juices flowing, you might write or draw in your journal, or talk about it with a trusted friend.
2. Select the above worry for this exercise, and write your own thoughts, beliefs, or feelings about it.
3. Underneath it, describe how this worry and its associated beliefs have caused trouble for you or your loved ones.
4. If you could grow beyond this worry, what would your life be like? How would it look and feel?

Examples

Gigi's Worry: *I'm never going to finish this book!*
My thoughts, beliefs, or feelings:
It will never be good enough. It's just too much work!

Consequences of holding these thoughts, beliefs, or feelings:
I am tense and preoccupied when I think I should be writing, so I rush through other activities without really enjoying them. I compare myself with other authors and feel even worse.

If I could grow beyond this worry, what would my life be like?
I could relax and enjoy myself when I'm not writing. I could be more compassionate with myself and accept that writing a book is not smooth or easy for anyone.

Second Worry: *I'm afraid to go to my high school reunion.*
Thoughts, beliefs, or feelings:
I'm depressed because I'm too fat. People will criticize me.

Consequences of holding these thoughts, beliefs, or feelings:
I'm eating to ease my stress. If I don't go, I'll feel terrible about missing everything.

If I could grow beyond this worry, what would my life be like?
I could relax and enjoy my friends without feeling self-conscious.

Third Worry: *I'm concerned my son is in a depression and he may have had a relapse.*
Thoughts, beliefs, or feelings:
I'm terrified and I have no idea what to do. I could never go on if something bad happened to him.

Consequences of holding these thoughts, beliefs, or feelings:
I'm so worried. I'm just stuck. I can't enjoy anything; I'm numbing myself out with overwork.

If I could grow beyond this worry, what would my life be like?
I would have supportive people around me. I would trust that we'll all be OK, regardless of the outcome. I could enjoy my life again.

After you complete the exercise, pat yourself on the back for taking the first steps toward freedom from your worries. If you find that looking so closely at your troubles is causing ongoing distress, please consult with a counselor, doctor, minister, or healthy friend.

Now that you've examined some of your whispered lies, let's see how *getting honest* can help you find peace, clarity, and connection.

Summary

- Whispered lies are responsible for the worries, fears, and unhappiness in your life. They block your wisdom, peace, and happiness.
- You can dissolve your worries by getting honest, claiming power, making choices, and using growth practices.
- The suggested tools focus your attention on peace and serenity. From this place, positive insights and solutions arise.
- Personal growth is best achieved by connecting periodically with others, be selective about the people you choose.

Chapter 2

GETTING HONEST ABOUT YOUR WORRIES
Strategy One

Lying to ourselves is more deeply ingrained
than lying to others.

—Fyodor Dostoevsky

What secrets have you been keeping from yourself? Perhaps you're worried about your own well-being or a loved one's overeating, overworking, drinking, or depression. Even though these worries occasionally get your attention, when they die down again, they're easy to forget.

The foundation of much unhappiness is *denial*, a coping mechanism that allows a person to reject a painful truth too uncomfortable to accept. Denial's voice emphatically whispers, "I don't want to admit the truth; and if I did, I just couldn't handle it."

As the saying goes, "We're only as sick as our secrets." All the concerns listed above, as well as binge eating, sleeping too much, obsessing about politics, or trying to control loved ones, are the unhealthy distractions of people in the grip of denial. In spite of these defenses, the pain hiding underneath the secret emerges, perhaps in a burst of outrage or in a bothersome sense of unrest in the gut. Tight shoulders, jaw clenching, headaches, frequent illness, and a host of other complaints may be symptoms of stifled truths and feelings.

For many of us, denial has been protective, softening the blows of life's pain with a cocoon of forgetting. But denial, when held onto for too long, can keep us from facing up to and learning from our experiences.

What Denial?

When I first heard Jane Stallings deliver a speech at Stanford University, her combination of charisma and intellect captivated me. Soon after, Jane hired me to organize her research studies of teacher improvement. For the next three years, this job helped pay my graduate school bills.

At the time, I was living with a rakish architect I'd met at a local bar. John was the last of four older men whom I had either married or lived with during my twenties and thirties. John and I would meet almost every night at the bar, drink a few beers, and visit with the regulars. Then we'd go home, get high, and make love to the sounds of Mozart or Sibelius.

This seemed like normal behavior to me, but not to Jane. She would often phone me in the evening about some work detail and find me less than coherent. She had also witnessed my bawdy behavior as John and I drank heavily at one of her dinner parties.

A few weeks after the party, Jane gently said, "You are such a talented woman and yet there's a piece in there that's just . . . I don't know, just not quite . . . " I can't recall her next words, but here's what I heard: "There's a part of you that's broken and it shows."

Jane's comment that day opened a tiny crack in my denial. It pierced my illusion that attracting men, earning good grades, and being well liked were hiding my pain. But I wasn't yet ready to question that illusion.

Later, Jane introduced me to Don, who would become my third husband. We fell in love quickly, and I moved to his home in Michigan to complete my dissertation. Don was a high school counselor, and he seemed to have his act together. From the very beginning, however, I tried to act exactly how I felt he wanted me to. This was my third marriage, and I didn't want to fail again.

After a year of living in this emotional pressure cooker, I found a drug dealer and began to get high, go to bars, and seek out attention from other men. Although filled with remorse each time, I couldn't resist the temptation.

One day, my manicurist invited me to her church. When the minister asked those who wanted to be saved to come forward, I marched up to the front of the line. I came home with new hope, flushed my drugs down the toilet, and vowed never to cheat on my husband again. But within a month, I was back to the drugs and booze. That's when I went to a tavern, picked up a stranger, and went home with him, as described in the preface.

Finally, Don suggested that I had a drinking problem. I defiantly replied I would prove him wrong by meeting with an alcoholism counselor. When the counselor said I was in the early stages of alcoholism, I foolishly thought with relief, "It can't be that bad." He then suggested I try having two drinks—no more and no less—each day, and take note of my behavior.

After a few months, I realized that while sometimes I could stop after two drinks, on other occasions, I would continue drinking, go home with a stranger, and cover up my actions with lies. When I honestly admitted that even after just one drink or drug I couldn't predict what would happen, my life began to change. I walked into my first Twelve-Step meeting one month before my thirty-eighth birthday. I've been clean and sober ever since.

Who's Not Good Enough?

Honestly facing the truth about myself was my last resort. When I was sufficiently disgusted by my own behavior, I was finally able to admit I had a problem. As I emerged from denial, I began to discover the many whispered lies and worries that were driving my self-destruction. "You are not good enough" was one of the most powerful.

My unconscious response to this belief had been to try with all my might to show everyone, including myself, that I *was* good enough. I spent many years inventing a "perfect self" by observing and imitating others who seemed happy.

My therapist called this strategy the *zero-sum* game. When I judged myself as less than someone else, I gave myself a minus 1. When I saw myself as better than someone else, I gave myself a plus 1. The sum of these two numbers is zero. Nobody wins.

In high school, I compared myself with the popular girls, judged myself as unworthy, and then began to imitate them. When they finally accepted me, I felt superior to the less popular girls (plus 1). When I got a good grade, I was on top of the world (plus 1). But when I received a low grade or criticism, I was devastated (minus 1).

Comparing myself to others set me up for a lifetime of debilitating perfectionism, one of my most painful survival strategies. One might say I became an egotist with an inferiority complex. I went back and forth between seeing myself as either the scum of the earth or far above others. There was no middle ground.

Why do we try so hard to create this perfect self? For those of us who grew up in troubled homes, it was a much-needed survival strategy. The irony is that the invented self does not bring long-term security or contentment. In fact, it plays havoc with most relationships, practically guaranteeing their failure. When you believe the only reason you are liked is because of who you are pretending to be, you fall prey to the whispered lie, "If he knew who I really am, he'd take one look and run in the opposite direction!"

Even more damaging, the invented self keeps you from knowing who *you* really are; therefore, you can't share with another what you truly feel or need. Without emotional honesty, your relationships founder on the shoals of boredom, frustration, or dysfunction.

Let's take a moment to examine some of your own central beliefs. The next exercise is called "two sides of the coin" because some of our most cherished strengths can occasionally interfere with happiness. One side of the coin is a good thing, but the other side might be harmful. Looking at both sides is one key to getting honest about the whispered lies that drive your worries.

Time for Action!
Tool 4. Two Sides of the Coin

The exercise below will help you examine your character strengths and their impact on your peace of mind. The first four rows are illustrations. In the first example, a woman notes, "I'm a good mother" as a personal strength with the benefit of caring well for her children. But a negative side to this strength may occur after her children leave home; she might constantly worry about them and find little pleasure in her life. She becomes a prisoner of the whispered lie, "If my children aren't safe and happy, I can't be content." As she addresses this negative belief with the Four Strategies and other tools, she has a good chance of overcoming her worry and depression.

1. Create three columns in your journal as in the example.
2. In the first column, list your personal strengths and the benefit of each one.
3. In the second column, list the ways in which each strength might be causing you stress or worry.
4. In the third column, try to identify the whispered lie driving each negative effect in your list.
5. Identify the false beliefs you want to work on as you read this book.

Example

Strengths and Benefits	Negative Effects	Whispered Lies (False Beliefs)
I'm a good mother. My children have been well cared for.	Now that they're gone, all I can do is worry about them.	If my children aren't safe and happy, I can't be content.
I'm a reliable employee. I'm successful at my job.	I work too many hours. My spouse says we have no time together.	I can't let up; I'll get fired.
I keep the peace at home. My spouse is happy. We don't fight.	I'm unhappy. I don't say what I need.	If I stand up for myself, my spouse will leave me.
I'm fashionable. I look attractive to others.	I spend a lot of time worrying about my appearance. I spend too much money on clothes.	If I'm not attractive, people won't like me. I'll be all alone.

Although we hold many whispered lies about ourselves, let's not forget our mind's tendency to blame others for our worries.

It's Not My Fault!

The *blame game* can keep people in a cycle of victim mentality. Think of the person who blames his parents for his low self-esteem. Driven by this whispered lie, he often repeats the same destructive patterns of behavior but expects different results. No growth occurs, just an endless series of disappointments.

We humans have a great tendency to avoid responsibility for our part in a difficult situation. Imagine you've just had a heated argument with your partner. As you replay the incident, your whispered lies tell you, "It's not my fault," "He should not have said that," or "If only he would be more understanding." While these statements might be partially true, this kind of blaming only keeps you stuck in worrying.

What if, instead of blaming him, you considered *your own part* in the disagreement? For example, you might discover you've been demanding, moody, or critical. You could then claim power, make choices, and use growth practices to overcome the false belief that your partner must be perfect. Once you're free of this whispered lie, you might find yourself focusing on his strengths instead of his faults. Perhaps you learn to state your own needs as preferences rather than demands. Eventually, your relationship begins to grow and thrive.

We all engage in denial or blame at one time or another. The important question is: How quickly can we see our own negative thinking and begin taking responsibility for it?

Time for Action!
Tool 5. Journal Writing or Drawing

Charles Raison and Vladimir Maletic report in *The New Mind-Body Science of Depression* that negative mental states are just as damaging to the heart as is smoking. Thus, getting honest about your own negativity is worth it; but it's not necessarily easy. One way to make an end run around the part of the mind in charge of denial is by writing or drawing as fast as possible. In *The Artist's Way*, best-selling author Julia Cameron suggests taking time every day to write or draw in a journal.

1. Select a situation that is troubling you as the focus for your writing or drawing.
2. Set a timer for five or ten minutes, or decide to stop when you fill three or four pages.
3. Write or draw freely, as fast as your hand can go. If you're writing, don't try to constrain yourself with any structure or judgments. If you're drawing, don't worry about the quality of your images. Just let your hand spontaneously record your thoughts and feelings.
4. After the time is up (or the pages are filled), take a minute to clarify what has emerged. Make notes about what you want to remember as you continue working through this book.
5. To help interpret what you've learned, you might talk to one or more of your growth partners (tool 2).
6. If you've uncovered something that seems too difficult to handle on your own, be sure to consult with a counselor or therapist.

It can be unsettling to admit that your whispered lies have been interfering with your happiness. But finding a new perspective about them can turn your worries around into a calm and healthy perspective.

The Deceit of Whispered Lies

Remember, most whispered lies distort the truth. Sonya Collins wrote in *WebMD*, "Stress is not a reaction to *an event* but rather to *how you interpret the event*." She uses the example of the false belief "If I don't work late every night, I'll get fired." Along with this belief goes the lie "I'm stuck and there's nothing I can do." Such beliefs increase the adrenaline flow of the fight-or-flight response. Over time, this causes the body to break down with stress symptoms such as chronic pain, bowel problems, and heart disease.

How can you change your interpretation of the events that worry you? One method is to question the truth of your whispered lies. For example, the man who believes he is stuck working long hours might challenge his belief, and then realize he is responsible for how much he works. From this point of honesty, he can begin to talk with others about how to change his situation. Perhaps he renegotiates his work schedule with his boss or delegates some of his work to others.

One of the whispered lies that recently caused me distress concerned Judy—my dear friend and business partner for over twenty years—who was diagnosed with breast cancer. In between her chemotherapy and multiple surgeries, she continued to work at her usual hectic pace. I was terrified Judy would get sick again, and I didn't want to lose her.

My worried mind whispered to me, "She should not work so much." Soon after admitting this, I began to seek a new way of looking at the situation. Just in time, a friend invited me to attend a weekend course with Byron Katie, the developer of The Work. Her book, *Loving What Is*, presents a powerful tool for examining and reframing the mind's negative interpretations.

Time for Action!
Tool 6. Is It True?

Byron Katie gave me permission to use this illustration of her process. My responses to the questions appear in italics. You may write your own responses, or reply aloud as a growth partner asks you the questions.

1. Write in your journal about a particularly troubling situation in your life. What's wrong? What should be different? *I am so worried about Judy. She's had cancer, and she's determined to work long hours even as she's recovering from surgery and chemotherapy. I'm terrified her ambitious work schedule will make her sick again. Nothing I say or do has changed the situation. I feel stuck.*

2. Select one thought to explore in greater depth. Write it at the top of a new page.
   Judy should not overwork.

3. Ask yourself, "Is this true?"
   Yes.

4. Ask yourself, "Can I absolutely know it's true?"
   No, probably not . . . there might be times when it's ok.

5. Ask yourself, "How do I react when I believe this thought?"
   I worry about Judy. I react by trying to do things for her. I judge her mistakes as being a result of her overwork. I'm thinking about this way too much, and it's robbing my peace of mind.

6. Ask yourself, "Who could I be if I didn't believe this thought? What might my life look like or feel like?"
   Without this thought, I'd be more accepting of how Judy is dealing with her illness. I could stop worrying about her and meddling in her life. I could relax.

7. Turn the thought around. What other ways of saying the original statement might be as true, or truer, than the original thought?
   Original statement: *Judy should not overwork.*
   - Turn the thought around to the opposite:
     *Judy **should** overwork.*
     In what way is this as true, or truer, than your original statement?
     She realizes every minute is precious and she has a lot she wants to do.
   - Turn the thought around to yourself:
     I should not overwork.
     In what way is this as true, or truer, than your original statement?
     I've been working too much and I'm under a lot of stress. I need to take better care of myself.

The point of this exercise is to see that the meaning you've constructed is not necessarily the truth. In my case, I was afraid Judy would get sick again, and I thought she would stay healthy if she worked less. When I turned it around, however, I saw that the decision was Judy's to make and not mine, that working might be exactly what she needed.

When I turned it around again, I got a big dose of honesty. I realized my true concern needed to be with *my own* overwork. As so often happens, when we point an accusing finger at another, we find three other fingers pointing back at us. This insight prompted me to face my own whispered lie that if I didn't work hard enough I would fail at my job. I had been worried about looking weak or imperfect, a hangover from my zero-sum-game days.

Whenever we detect false beliefs interfering with our serenity, it's time to take a breath and acknowledge the scary unpredictability of life. Then we can use the Four Strategies and other tools to face our challenges with courage and grace.

You Can Make It!

What can we learn from people who are able to find peace in the midst of their difficulties? What distinguishes them from those who remain prisoners of their negative beliefs? Brené Brown's research, reported in *The Gifts of Imperfection,* found that such people share four characteristics: They trust they'll learn something valuable; connect with loving friends; practice self-compassion; and are patient with their difficult situations.

Seeing your own worries as opportunities to grow is a powerful choice—one you made when you picked up this book and began to apply the tools. The second characteristic, joining with growth partners, was discussed at the end of chapter 1, We Can't Do It Alone.

Treating oneself with compassion and patience, the last two of the four characteristics, are of great importance when facing life's challenges. Their opposites are condemnation and resistance. These evil foes tell us what we're experiencing is horribly wrong, and even worse, that *it is our fault.* But, instead of believing this lie and blaming ourselves, we need to do the opposite: practice self-compassion.

During my tough times, I now try to accept myself exactly as I am at that moment. When I revert to old patterns and fears, I remind myself that growth is gradual with both progress and setbacks. I often imagine myself holding up a sign that says, "Under construction. Pardon my dust!" At other times, I repeat to myself, "Progress, not perfection."

I had an opportunity to learn about self-care and patience when I was disabled in my late forties with adhesive capsulitis, a painful condition where my shoulders froze and I couldn't raise my arms higher than my chest. For three years, I tried every available cure but continued to suffer. I could barely drive my car or write by hand. I even had to cut my hair very short (horrors!) because I couldn't use a hairdryer.

At first, I resisted this seemingly unending experience. Then one day, as I was complaining about my condition, a dear friend suggested I listen to Pema Chodron's CD, *Good Medicine*. Chodron, an American Buddhist nun and prolific author, spoke with humor and wisdom about practicing compassion towards ourselves as we feel emotions we'd rather not feel— for instance, pain, confusion, fear, sadness, or shame. She explained that denial, worry, and impatience do not help because they distract us from what we need most—nurturing self-care.

As I listened to her words, I had a moment of clarity. I had been judging myself harshly by believing the whispered lie, "I should be able to handle this pain with grace and patience; I shouldn't be so upset and worried" (minus 1!). I realized I needed to give myself the same comforting words I'd give to a cherished friend or sister with a distressing illness. For example, I could think, "I'm sorry this is so hard. What can we do to make it easier?" When I focused on self-caring thoughts rather than self-punishing ones, I began to make changes. I cut back on my work, rested more often, and asked my friends and family for help.

Understanding your own character can be a great aid to gaining self-compassion. If you're exceptionally prone to worry, easily overwhelmed, and feel things very deeply, you might be a *highly sensitive person*. Elaine Aron's twenty-five years of research indicates that about one-fifth of the U.S. population is highly sensitive to external stimuli, reflects on things more than others, and prefers quiet, less chaotic surroundings. They are also more emotionally reactive than others.

If you are highly sensitive, others may have told you that you're too "high-maintenance" or "thin-skinned." I've certainly had those labels applied to me. You'll be happy to hear that the characteristics of highly sensitive people are highly valued in many societies. In fact, these sensitive ones often become the wise advisors to the community. The healthiest path for those like us is to accept who we are and take good care of ourselves.

Since honestly facing yourself and taking responsibility for your life can be tough, it's important to learn how to be kind to yourself.

Time for Action!
Tool 7. Self-Compassion

Dr. Kristin Neff's research, reported in *Self-Compassion*, indicates that compassion for yourself is an essential characteristic of resilient, healthy people. I use her guided meditations whenever I'm feeling stuck in negativity, and they never cease to free me. Take a few minutes to experience the healing force of Neff's words.

1. Download the app called Insight Timer and click on the headphone icon at the bottom of the screen.
2. Search for "Kristin Neff" or "self-compassion."
3. Listen to one of the guided meditations and follow along.
4. Congratulate yourself for taking time to cultivate kindness toward yourself.

You've just experienced the peaceful healing of a guided meditation. For some of the time, you were probably completely absorbed in the experience, without concerns about the past or the future. This is called *being in the present moment.*

Right Here. Right Now.

They say that the past is over and the future is yet to be. The only thing that remains is the present moment. A powerful way to gain peace of mind and valuable information about ourselves is to be in the now. This idea, recently popularized in Eckhart Tolle's best seller, *The Power of Now*, relates closely to the idea of mindfulness we examined in chapter 1.

Dr. Jon Kabat-Zinn, the developer of mindfulness-based programs, teaches people to fully appreciate the present by asking them to take several minutes to eat one raisin. As they chew, they savor the full sensory experience—the texture, taste, and sound. Try it now.

If you don't have a raisin, wash a few dishes very slowly. Feel the texture of each one. Listen to the sounds they make as they clink together. Smell the moist air lingering around you. When you mindfully immerse yourself in the present moment, you can feel your mind unhinge from all the distressing thoughts about your past and future.

During the second year of my constant shoulder pain, I bought Chodron's popular book, *When Things Fall Apart.* I was struck by her suggestion that one could attain peace by simply being present with each moment, even the distressing ones. When I first read this statement, I thought, "Is she crazy? Who would want to linger in the 'now' of their discomfort? I want to get rid of it, not embrace it!"

After I reflected on this idea, I realized that during my illness, my mind had never considered finding resolution in the present. I had been searching through my *past* actions, worrying about what I'd done to make my shoulders worse. When I wasn't dwelling on the past, I was trying to figure out what treatment to try in the *future.*

I was desperate enough to try Chodron's suggestion to suspend my judging thoughts and be present with my body's sensations. As I continued this practice, I felt loving healing flow into my life to dissolve my worry and self-condemnation. Even though my shoulders didn't heal immediately, I was able to handle the pain and limitations with much greater peace. Today both of my shoulders are flexible and strong thanks, in part, to surgery. Every time I reach overhead with ease and comfort, I am grateful for my healed body.

Since you can't worry when you're immersed in the now, you'll want to learn this skill. It's merely a matter of consistent practice, somewhat like training a dog to sit and stay. When your mind wants to race away from the current reality, give it gentle encouragement to return to observing the sensations of the present moment. It's similar to Tool 1, Mindfulness Meditation in chapter 1.

Tuning into your body's messages can be a great aid to honesty. In *Kitchen Table Wisdom*, Rachel Naomi Remen describes a woman whose chest would feel tight occasionally with a mild angina attack. Over time, she realized she had this pain whenever she was dishonest with herself, for example, when she pretended to enjoy an activity her husband liked but she didn't care for. She soon came to rely on her body's signal that she needed to express herself more honestly. As she did so, her relationships with her loved ones improved.

Let's take a moment to examine the focus of your thoughts.

Time for Action!
Tool 8. The Balcony View

Taking the *balcony view*, a term coined by Marty Linsky and Ron Heifetz of Cambridge Leadership Associates, is a powerful technique for rising above the fray to gain a fresh perspective. In this exercise, we'll use the balcony view to discover if your focus is on the past, present, or future.

1. Imagine you're sitting in the balcony at a theater, watching yourself on the stage. The acoustics allow you to hear distinctly each of your own thoughts.
2. Begin thinking about a current challenge in your life.
3. Set a timer and monitor your thoughts for one minute. In your journal, jot down on a separate line every thought as it comes to you.
4. When the time is up, read your list and put a P next to the ones about the *past* and an F next to the ones about the *future*.
5. What patterns do you notice? What might you want to change?

When I first did this exercise, I was amazed to see I had put a P or an F next to almost every thought I had! Perhaps you did, too. Examining what I wrote also helped me see the past and future issues occupying my mind.

Worrying about the future or past rarely yields a remedy. In fact, it's often just a way of denying present circumstances and, therefore, not taking responsibility for them. As Corrie ten Boom, savior of many Jews during World War II, wrote, "Worry does not empty tomorrow of its sorrow; it empties today of its strength." Since this present moment is all you really have, immerse yourself in it.

After reading about honesty, self-compassion, and being in the now, some of you might be wondering, "Isn't being present with my feelings the same as wallowing in them?" or "Isn't self-compassion just the same as self-pity?" You might worry you'll lose your effectiveness at work or home if you "go soft" on yourself. You may even see all this honest self-examination as a waste of time.

As you keep reading through this book, I hope you'll realize that self-honesty is the most important of the Four Strategies. After all, if you remain in denial of your true feelings and beliefs, how can you ever change their results?

As you try the recommended tools in this chapter, your mind might whisper, "I'm failing at this," or "Others can do this so easily, why can't I?" Remember that you're only at the beginning. It's going to take practice and patience to overcome a lifetime of habitual worry. The good news is: Underneath your whispered lies is your very own heart of gold.

According to most wisdom traditions, every one of us has a source of *power* that can overcome the patterns and worries that keep us stuck. Your true self is good. If this idea seems like a stretch to you, please suspend your disbelief and consider the ideas offered in chapter 3.

Summary

- Self-honesty is the first step toward overcoming worry.
- You may have pretended to be someone that you perceived others wanted you to be so you could gain friends, prestige, and/or romance.

- When you fail to achieve your dreams and happiness, you've likely denied your part in your problems or blamed others.
- Your mind's interpretations of your current circumstances are often in error. Fortunately, you can choose a different perspective.
- Practicing patience and compassion toward yourself helps you overcome worry.
- Focusing on the present moment is a powerful way to learn from your experiences.

Chapter 3

CLAIMING POSITIVE POWER
Strategy Two

*A mystic sees beyond the illusion of separateness into
the intricate web of life in which all things are expressions of a
single Whole. You can call this web God, the Tao, the Great
Spirit, the Infinite Mystery, Mother or Father,
but it can be known only as love.*
　　　　　　　—Joan Z. Borysenko, *Pocketful of Miracles*

Have you ever repeatedly tried to get someone or something to change? It
might be a child, spouse, in-law, parent, or a political issue. Perhaps your
mind has encouraged your futile attempts by whispering, "I know I can
fix (*fill in the blank*) so we can be happy."

Whispered lies such as "I must make this better," and "I don't want
that experience" have no power to produce true happiness. In fact, they
create the opposite: worry, distress, judging, and incessant negative
thinking.

Take a moment to question the effectiveness of your own willpower.
How well has trying to control others worked for you? Do you believe you
can impose the changes you'd like to see in the world? Perhaps you've
tried some of the activities in chapter 2, and realized how hard it is to
change even your own thinking.

When you honestly admit your personal will can't fulfill your desires,
a wondrous alternative appears. I call it *positive power*. This power helps
you find peace and courage, no matter what's going on in your life. And

it works: Studies reported by Stephanie Castillo in *Prevention* reveal that believers in such a power are happier than those who don't believe.

If you're one of the many people skeptical about a positive power, let me assure you: I won't suggest you worship any particular spiritual entity, religion, dogma, or philosophy. You'll be defining this source in a way that works for you. You can be as unconventional or traditional as you want *as long as you tap into something greater than your fears.*

As you learned in the preface, claiming a source of positive power helped me overcome my lifelong insecurities, worries, and negative patterns. It can do the same for you.

I'm Not Safe!

Around the time I was nine or ten, I began to have horrible anxiety, a fear I could not name or understand. When my best friend, Polly, invited me to attend church with her, I eagerly went, hoping religion would give me some relief. Perhaps the prayers I said during services and the songs I sang in choir would save me from feeling deep inside that I was bad. I even joined a youth group where I earned tiny metal feathers for memorizing the names of the chapters in the Bible. As I hooked each feather onto a small pin, I hoped for a miracle to end my misery.

As I grew older, my budding sexuality was in direct conflict with my search for salvation. In junior high, I discovered the thrill of making out with my boyfriend; and when I was fourteen, I developed a crush on a twenty-five-year-old man. As we lay in the backseat of his car, I felt an even greater surge of sensual excitement. Fortunately, he moved away before we went further.

My fears and confusion led me to join Young Life, a Christian nondenominational organization. At first, attending meetings was a great excuse to get out of the house on a school night. When I went to a Young Life camp in Colorado, the leaders encouraged us to grasp the wonder of God's creation, an easy sell with the majestic Rocky Mountains surrounding us. As the week progressed, however, the camp leaders upped the ante by telling us three things we must to do to avoid going to hell.

First, we had to admit and reject our sins. I was playing with sex in every way I could without experiencing the actual act. Giving it up was a tall order. Second, we should accept Jesus as our personal savior. That requirement made all my "bullshit detectors" go off. Why did I need a savior? I was popular, got good grades, and had a boyfriend. Wasn't that enough? Inside, a not-so-small voice said it wasn't. But I couldn't yet heed that wisdom.

The third condition was to turn our lives over to God's guidance. Given my failure to accept the first two conditions, the third was not an option. My adolescent mind imagined I might end up as a nun! In spite of my reservations, I kept attending Young Life events; I even joined a prayer group.

When I went to college, I started dating Brian. The passion of our romance and my burgeoning drinking career blocked all further interest in religion. After Brian left for the Air Force, I went to a party at his fraternity and drank rum punch all night. The next thing I knew, I was off to have sex in a hotel room with Brian's fraternity brother. Afterward, each of us lied to conceal our betrayal of Brian.

It took several more years of living with my addictions to admit my way of running my life was yielding disastrous results. After I surrendered, I was told a power greater than myself could restore me to sane behavior. Based on my earlier attempts, I wasn't so sure *anything* could help me, but I was desperate enough to give it a try.

A Power Greater Than Worry

I had my first inkling of a positive power after following a meditation teacher's suggestion that I sit quietly, observe my thoughts, and then ask myself, "Right now, who is watching my thinking?" The question stopped me in my tracks. I wondered, "If I *am* my thoughts—which I believed up until that point—how could *another part of me* be observing them?" And, yet, there I was, watching my mind be amazed by this astounding idea. For the first time, I realized there must be some part of me that is greater than my thoughts.

How any of us come to understand this power is highly personal and our business only. You may find it in your mind, spirit, body energy, or in the universe. Perhaps you'll discover it through the hope and strength of supportive healthy people. Consider carefully what they say and how they live their lives. Then take what works for you and leave the rest behind.

Time for Action!
Tool 9. Your Positive Power

Finding a better way to handle hardship, stress, or trauma undoubtedly brought you to this book. Researcher Brené Brown found that people who cope well with such challenges believe they are "connected to each other by a power greater than all of us." Now is your chance to identify a power that can dissolve your worries and bring you happiness.

1. Take a minute to ponder what kind of power could bring goodness into your life.
2. Read the common names for a source of a positive power in figure 3.1. Pause to notice which ones, if any, feel right for you.
3. When making your choice, consider where you imagine this power to be. Could it be a source within you, a true self? A higher power above you? The infinite universal intelligence around you?
4. Select a few names that work for you. Circle them, write them down, or hold them in your heart.
5. If your past taught you to be fiercely independent, it may take a while to trust this power. But stick with it and you'll reap the rewards.

To reduce confusion, I use the terms *positive power* and *loving power* in this book. When you encounter these words, feel free to substitute the names you've selected. As you use the tools offered in these chapters, you will come to understand this power more and more, regardless of what you call it.

Abba	Inner Guide
Adonai	Healer
Allah	Jehova/Jesus
Angels	Light
Being	Mary
Buddha	Nature's Perfection
Christ, Holy Spirit, Jesus	Oneness
Courage	Perfect Order
Divine Mind	Positive Attitudes and Beliefs
Energy	Providence
God (Good Orderly Direction)	Ram
Great Spirit	Shiva
Guardian Angel	Sophia (feminine deity)
Healing Energy/Resonance	Source
Higher Power	Tao
Higher Self	True Self
Holy Father	Wisdom
Infinite/Universal Intelligence	Yahweh

Figure 3.1 Names for Positive Power

Love Is Stronger Than Fear

One day, after telling my friend I had been struggling to believe in a loving power, she suggested, "Just fake it till you make it." I responded, "Really? Fake it till you make it? I always thought faith was a concrete thing you either had or didn't have." "No. It's a decision," she said. "You *make a choice* whether to give this power a chance."

I wondered if I *did* fake it—by acting as if a positive power were real, even if I had no proof of its existence—would it make me happier?

Possibly. Would it be self-deception? Maybe. Did I care? No. At that moment, I had a tiny amount of willingness to experiment with this new power. And that was enough.

Years before, I had asked Jane Stallings, my grad school mentor, what helped her remain so calm and collected with her professional and family challenges. She replied that she studied *A Course in Miracles* (ACIM), a text that helps readers overcome fear and judgment through love's power.

Soon after I arrived in Michigan, Jane sent me Gerald Jampolsky's book, *Love Is Letting Go of Fear*, which pared down ACIM's complex text into a small number of teachings. When I picked it up, I began to learn about the serene power I admired in Jane. Soon after, I was fascinated by the ideas in Marianne Williamson's best seller, *A Return to Love: Reflections on The Principles of A Course in Miracles*.

Many of the world's wisdom traditions (a term used by author and spiritual leader, Deepak Chopra) teach this single lesson: Our most important choice is to *align our thoughts and actions with love rather than with fear.* Consider the following truths from *ACIM.*

- *We are spiritual beings living inside a physical body.* The confusion of the human experience comes from thinking our body represents the full extent of our being. The true essence of a person, however, is not the body. It is the spirit, also known as the soul, positive power, love, true self, and so on. Most of us seek to connect with a loving source of safety, comfort, and wisdom.
- *Fear separates us.* When we believe we are merely a physical body, we think there isn't enough love, attention, or material security to go around. We live in fear as we constantly compete against others to fulfill our human needs. In this survival state, we separate ourselves from one another. ACIM and many other teachings refer to this self-centered fear as the *ego,* and consider it the main source of unhappiness. (Freud defined the ego differently—as the decision-making part of the personality.)

- *Love connects us.* When love (positive power) is our driving force, we trust there is enough of everything we need to be happy and secure. We connect with others in loving care and compassion. We are no longer driven by our fears and we find joy.

To simplify: Fear, judgment, and separation create worries. Loving connections cure them.

It's sometimes difficult to determine whether we're being guided by love or fear. At such times, we can pause and ask, "Am I (or they) coming from a place of fear which might be disguised as love?" Unfortunately, human instincts to dominate events and other people often mask themselves as loving gestures. If others try to control you in any way, they may be operating out of their own fear rather than compassion. In turn, your tendency to judge another provides an opportunity to reject this belief and see him with only love.

This brings us to an interesting question: Can you access positive power through other people? I believe so. In fact, that's the way most of us in Twelve-Step programs first felt this benevolent force. The people there had no selfish agenda; they saw beyond my shameful past into my true goodness. Their kind regard and wise words showed me a loving power I had never known.

You too can share your life challenges and solutions with positive people. I suggest meeting weekly with one or two others who fit the characteristics listed in Who's a Good Growth Partner? at the end of chapter 1. Perhaps you could read this book or another that you find inspiring. As you continue to meet, you'll likely experience the positive power of connection. To paraphrase: Where two or more are gathered in loving purpose, amazing things happen.

Choosing goodness over fear definitely pays off. In the *Journal of Personality and Social Psychology*, Barbara Fredrickson and her colleagues confirm that immersing yourself in feelings of love and appreciation lowers depressive symptoms and increases life satisfaction. Try the following two simple tools to experience these benefits.

Time for Action!
Tool 10. Focusing on Loved Ones

Think about the joy you feel when you focus on a person or pet you love—not the manic high of romantic love, but one more solid and enduring.

1. Bring to mind someone you hold dear and with whom you are at peace, perhaps your child, grandchild, sister, brother, dear friend, or spouse. If you have a four-legged child as I do, it might be your kitty or puppy. If possible, directly observe or look at a picture of your loved one.
2. Breathe in and out slowly, feeling love filling your mind and heart as you ponder the one you cherish.
3. Continue breathing and directing your attention to the experience of love.
4. Your feeling of peaceful joy and appreciation reflects positive power.

One day as I watched my little gray kitten, Murphy, purring on my lap, I felt so much love for her. I wondered if my positive power might feel that same sweet love for me. It was then I realized that I could invite this love to fill the gaping holes I felt inside me.

Time for Action!
Tool 11. Appreciating Beauty

The power of beauty is all around you. Take time to look, feel, taste, and listen to the parts of the world that speak to your heart. I feel my fears drop away when I listen to my favorite music. You may find that nature does the same for you. As Sir Thomas Browne said, "All things are artificial, for *nature is the art of God.*"

1. Select one of these to enjoy:
   - A piece of music or song you love;
   - A passage in a book or a poem that lifts your heart; or
   - A picture, painting, or place that gives you pleasure.

2. Take a few minutes to immerse yourself in this beauty. Breathe it in. Relax into it. Feel your heart expand. Keep focusing on this feeling.
3. Rest. Be still. Give thanks.
4. Look up and notice how the world looks to you now.

As you diligently seek experiences that lift your spirits, you'll increase your conscious contact with goodness.

Cuddle Up to Your Power

How can you put your positive power to work in your life? By making a single decision again and again: Reject your fear-filled whispered lies and connect with your source of power. As you continue making this choice, you will discover a new outlook and intuitive guidance for your problems.

One of the simplest ways to access your loving power is to offer kindness to someone else. If you're down in the dumps, try doing something nice for another person that doesn't involve giving advice or fixing them. It only requires that you say or do something kind without an agenda or expectations. Such acts of generosity wash away fear and expand happiness in all lives.

Time for Action!
Tool 12. Acts of Kindness

In *Living an Inspired Life*, Wayne Dyer cites evidence that merely extending a kindness to another improves the immune system and increases the brain's production of the feel-good substance serotonin. Surprisingly, a person who simply *observes* an act of kindness receives similar benefits.

1. Think about an experience where someone has done a kind act for another. It may be a small act (letting a car enter traffic) or a large one (giving millions to a charity). It's impossible to quantify love.

2. Imagine the person's heart shining brightly as he gives care and consideration to someone else.
3. Now choose to do or say something nice for another, even if it's simply offering a sincere smile to someone you see on the street. Or you might thank a waiter or cashier for doing a good job. As the person receives your appreciation, feel the joy of loving connection.

Recently I heard a spiritual teacher say, "A smile, given to anyone, is a prayer." But, what if you don't feel like smiling at someone? How can you start your day on a positive note?

Tool 13. Inspirational Reading

Reading inspirational texts each morning connects you with a positive power. You might spend time with Buddhist teachings, the Bible, or any other resource that appeals to you. (Some of my favorites are listed in appendix C.) I like meditation books that contain a short reading and a prayer or affirmation for each day of the year. I also read a lesson from *A Course in Miracles* every day. It's one of the best ways of reprogramming my mind away from fear and toward love.

Simply read or listen to your selection; then think (or write) about how you might apply it in your life. If difficulties begin to fill your day, you can use any of your favorite growth tools to start down a better path.

As you clear your mind and open yourself to messages that speak to your heart, helpful resources often appear in surprising ways. For example, you might hear about a certain book several times in the same month. When a tool comes to you this way, it's likely to be the right one for you.

Tool 14. Prayer

Admittedly, I did a lot of faking it when it came to prayer, but I persisted and found it works. Prayer puts loving power into the driver's seat of your life. Ask anyone who prays regularly, and they'll tell you they feel more peaceful and happy.

Choose a prayer that appeals to you. You don't have to direct it to any specific source, just send it to something bigger and wiser than you. You can pray first thing in the morning or at any time you wish. You don't have to kneel or fold your hands. Nothing is required other than your desire to find a new approach to life.

You might wonder what happens if you don't believe what you're saying. Try to think of prayer in this way: Even if you are just mouthing the words, your recognition of a positive power certainly has a better chance of improving your situation than a steady diet of negativity.

Since we don't always know what's best for others or ourselves, we'd be wise to avoid specific requests. Instead, we pray for a positive outlook and intuitive guidance.

Deb Engle suggests the only little prayer you'll ever need is "Please heal my fear-based thoughts." Another prayer that covers just about everything is Reinhold Niebuhr's Serenity Prayer. It may be right for you.

> *God grant me the serenity to accept the things I cannot change,*
> *Courage to change the things I can,*
> *And wisdom to know the difference.*

The Serenity Prayer asks your positive power to help you peacefully accept those things over which you have no power, and to have the courage to change what you can. In my experience, this usually means changing only myself—my whispered lies, words, and actions. Wisdom helps you pause and consider which of the two choices is the best for your situation.

You might wonder why you need a source of wisdom to help you figure out what you can or can't change. To understand this idea, take a moment to remember the damage done when you tried to force a change outside of your control.

I did some damage when I talked to my sister's husband about how his drinking harmed her. After learning this, she said, "I wish you had trusted that I was strong enough to take care of this myself." She was right. I didn't wait for the wisdom to decide whether to accept the situation or intervene. I just went ahead and talked to him. I paid a big price for my error; it took a long time for my sister to confide in me again.

Time for Action!
Tool 14. The Serenity Prayer

Think of a worrisome situation you'd like to change. In my case, it's trying to get my husband to exercise. My motives are good. I know he'd be healthier and more comfortable, and I sure would like him to live longer! The Serenity Prayer helps me detach from the whispered lie that it's my responsibility to get my husband to exercise.

1. Notice every time you think or speak about your problem. For example, I feel anxious and angry as I think, "Oh no! He's gaining weight." Or I might say, in a kind but controlling voice, "Honey, why don't you take a walk?"
2. Whenever you catch yourself pondering how to fix your situation, STOP! Leave it in your mind and don't act. Say the Serenity Prayer (or another positive phrase) and keep saying it until your worry and need for control fade away.
3. Repeat step 2 as often as necessary. (This could be a lot!)
4. Eventually, you will find yourself either completely unconcerned about the problem, or you will intuitively know what to say or do *when the time is right*. Many people use the *three-day rule*; they wait three days to gain perspective before taking action, and if still uncertain about how to respond, they wait three more days.

It may seem naïve to believe that changing what you think can have such a profound effect on your happiness, but it does.

You Can Change Your Mind!

As scientist Joe Dispenza, author of *Evolve Your Brain*, writes, brain science is the contemporary language of mysticism. The brain is where both our fearful and loving attitudes live, encoded in neural pathways. The content of these cognitive programs determines whether we perceive the world around us as essentially safe or threatening.

The great news is that intentionally cultivating loving thoughts, good feelings, and positive experiences can reprogram the brain's negative wiring. As the author and teacher Emmet Fox wrote in *The Sermon on The Mount*, "You cannot think one thing and produce another."

Here's a summary of how our brains work:

- Our life events, especially the emotionally charged ones, create neural programs in our brains.
- By the time we're in our mid- to late-thirties, 90 percent of our mental pathways have been constructed.
- Each time we replay a thought or emotion—either internally or aloud—we strengthen its negative or positive neural pathway.
- The brain uses its past programming to interpret new situations. It then reacts as it did in the past *even when the new situation is not the same at all.*

One of my favorite lessons in *A Course in Miracles* is, "I'm never upset for the reason I think." In my experience, I'm usually upset because I believe an old whispered lie that appears to apply to my present situation. When I honestly examine this belief, I can choose to free myself from its tyranny.

For example, when I was a little girl and made a mistake, my father said, "Gigi, how can you be so goddamn dumb!" For years, whenever I faced a challenge, that old whispered lie told me I wasn't smart enough to overcome it. In spite of this fear, I was able to succeed in my career, but with a great deal of stress.

Shortly after I got sober, I flew to Denver to receive a writing award from a national education organization. After the MC called my name, I walked up to receive the plaque and turned to hear loud applause. To my astonishment, all I felt was embarrassment. My face turned bright red and I muttered, "Thank you," followed by a few incoherent words. I felt horrible.

I had expected to feel wonderful as I was recognized for my accomplishment, but I had only felt confused. With the help of my therapist, I was able to find the "I am dumb" program my father had instilled in me. When the reality of my national award confronted this false belief, my mind couldn't reconcile the two, and I froze.

Later work with my therapist convinced me that my future did not need to be driven by old whispered lies. I could begin to act as if they didn't exist. For example, he taught me to receive praise with a smile and a confident thank you rather than discounting compliments. He also recommended I use the techniques in David Burns's book, *Feeling Good: The New Mood Therapy*, a popular publication about cognitive change.

One of the most powerful ways to restructure negative thinking is by acquiring gratitude. Think of it as *wanting what you have* instead of *yearning for what you don't have.* In my case, I chose to give thanks to my editor and myself for the effort we put into the award-winning article instead of worrying about how I responded to the applause.

Time for Action!
Tool 15. Gratitude List

The simple act of shifting one's mind toward gratitude has been shown to positively impact health, stress, and sleep quality. Robert A. Emmons's *Thanks! How Practicing Gratitude Can Make You Happier* summarizes these research findings. Try the exercise below to gain an attitude of gratitude.

1. In your journal, make a list of five things for which you are grateful.
2. Read them one at a time. After each one, pause to notice how you feel.
3. Look at the world around you. What do you see? Doom and gloom or the bright possibility of goodness?
4. Every day, read your gratitude list and add five *new items* to it without repeating any of them.
5. When you catch yourself worrying, shift your thoughts to your growing gratitude list.

As you consistently use this practice, you'll find it dissolves many of your most negative beliefs. You'll begin to see people and situations in a more positive light.

Now that you're considering that there's a power greater than your own worries, what's next? You have an important *choice* to make: How will you put your honesty and positive power into action to benefit both yourself and others?

Summary

- When you honestly look at your troubling situations, it's important to admit that the way you've been running things isn't working, and you need to find a different way.
- You don't need to intellectually understand a positive power for it to work for you.
- Fear and judgment keep you upset and alone; a loving power overcomes your fear and connects you to others.
- It takes time and practice to trust your positive power to bring you peace and happiness.
- Research on neuroscience supports the power of the mind for positive change.

Chapter 4

CHOOSING A NEW FUTURE
Strategy Three

> *It's important to understand that we are responsible for*
> *cultivating the kind of personalities we have every minute*
> *we're present in this world.*
> —Karen Casey, *Meditations on the Course*

Doing nothing is a decision to stay stuck in the misery of your worries and whispered lies; if nothing changes, nothing changes. Are you willing to take the necessary actions to become your best self? If so, you'll be making three crucial choices:

- *Choice 1. Declare your dream or intention.* What's your vision of who you want to be in your life?
- *Choice 2. Let go of attachment to the outcome.* Will you trust—even a little bit—that your positive power can help you achieve your wishes in a way that yields the highest good for all, even if it's in an unexpected way?
- *Choice 3. Get to work with growth tools.* Will you direct your mind away from your negative thinking and toward loving power, so your desired outcome—or something better—will occur?

Of course, it's important to set goals; but have you ever noticed your plans don't always work out the way you intended? You might then wonder why you should even set a goal if you're not going to get exactly what you want. Remember that in chapter 3 you claimed a source of power to overcome your fears and worries. When you stay connected to this power, you can hold your desire loosely, allowing room for it to manifest in the best manner and timing.

This does not mean, however, that you can't do anything constructive in a difficult situation. You can, if you remain aware that your best decisions will come from a peaceful state of mind. Pausing to mindfully meditate (tool 1) or say the Serenity Prayer (tool 14) will help you know which actions to take and which ones *not* to take.

Here's how I made three powerful choices to fulfill my dream of having a happy and stable marriage.

My Dream Comes True

After I quit using alcohol and drugs to drown my feelings, I was left with the empty truths of my life. Even my educational and career accomplishments couldn't diminish the pain I felt from my failed marriages. Following a year of couples therapy, my third husband, Don, and I divorced. I was convinced I simply lacked the ability to love and would never be happily married. When I got honest about this whispered lie and claimed the power to overcome it, I was ready to choose a future honoring my hope to be happily married.

When I shared this dream with a friend, she suggested I write my intention in my journal and focus on it repeatedly. I wrote, "I want to be healthy and happy in a relationship with a man." A few weeks later, I learned to make my affirmation stronger by stating it as if it were already done. So, I rewrote the words on a sticky note and put it on my bathroom mirror. Every time I noticed it, I repeated aloud, "Thank you, positive power, for my healthy and happy relationship with a man."

Another friend recommended I place a copy of my intention in a small box. (My friends call it a "God box" or "miracle box".) Whenever I found myself dwelling on my failed marriages, I remembered that by placing my wish in that box, I had chosen to let my positive power fulfill it.

My past had taught me I shouldn't make this goal my top priority. For the rest of that year, I stayed away from romance and kept my focus on staying sober, developing relationships with healthy women, and trusting my positive power. During that time, my therapist helped me uncover and heal the lies that had brought me so much heartbreak: "I'm not worthy of love," and "I must be perfect to be loved."

When I returned from spending Christmas with my parents, I was feeling a bit of postholiday letdown, so I went to a Twelve-Step meeting to bolster my sobriety. After seeing that every chair was occupied, I sat on the floor. But I couldn't find a comfortable position since I had hurt my back a few weeks before. One of the men noticed my discomfort and offered me his chair.

After the meeting, someone suggested we all go out for coffee. As I sat quietly, enjoying the friendly banter, I noticed the man who had given me his seat. Peter had striking hazel eyes and an easy manner as he enthusiastically showed everyone a Christmas gift he'd received. It was a digital business card that could store phone numbers. When he passed it to me, I daringly put my name and phone number in it. Later, when he asked if I'd like to go to a movie sometime, I said yes. He didn't need to request my number.

Soon we were going out regularly, but I was cautious. In contrast to my former relationships, I didn't make Peter the center of my life. In fact, I limited myself to seeing him only twice a week so I could attend meetings, go to therapy, meet with friends, and continue my journaling, affirmations, and prayer.

Six months later, when I realized I was falling in love with him, I found myself in tears, terrified I would repeat my past mistakes. I talked to my therapist and prayed diligently. I continued to take things slowly, rededicated myself to my program, and kept repeating my affirmation, "Thank you, positive power, for my healthy and happy relationship with a man."

As I grew to trust the wisdom of my loving power, I realized I shouldn't get too specific about my requests, so I added the words, "in the best way for all involved." Adding this language indicated my willingness for a man other than Peter to be my future partner.

Gradually, I faced and changed the patterns that had sabotaged my prior relationships. I learned to honestly identify and express my feelings to Peter. I gave up pretending to be perfect, and started to believe he and others could accept me exactly as I was.

Two years later, we married. The fact we recently celebrated our twenty-eighth anniversary demonstrates how wonderfully those choices turned out.

The affirmation I wrote on that sticky note lives on, tattered and soiled, in the bottom of my makeup basket. Every so often, I see it there and give thanks for the miracle of our happy marriage.

Everyone deserves miracles. Applying these same three choices to your life will help you find yours.

Choice 1.
Declare Your Dream

Can you trust a positive power to draw good things into your life? If you need a little convincing, consider the history of this idea. In 1952, Norman Vincent Peale's influential book, *The Power of Positive Thinking,* sold over five million copies, and many claimed it changed their lives for the better. Fifty years later, renowned psychologist Martin Seligman wrote that positive people have better health, longevity, sociability, and success (research summarized in *Authentic Happiness: Using the New Positive Psychology to Realize Your Potential for Lasting Fulfillment).*

It's clear that carefully directing your thinking can change your life. The first step is to write an affirmation using the following guidelines.

- *Use the present tense.* State your desire as if it has already happened: "I am relaxed, smart, and successful when I take my exam," "I see (*fill in the blank*) without criticism and offer kindness instead."
- *Use positive language.* Make your statement affirmative: "I have strong flexible shoulders." Avoid all negative language; for

example, replace "I am not in pain," with "I am free of pain and enjoy good health."

- *Use concrete and emotionally powerful terms.* The affirmation, "My marriage is strong, loving, honest, and wonderful!" arouses confident, optimistic feelings.
- *Make it open to love's direction.* Add the words, "in the best way for all involved," or "as positive power would have it be."

"I write wonderful books in a wonderful way. I offer wonderful service for wonderful pay," are the affirmations that have been helping me write this book. I adapted them from an example in Florence Scovel Shinn's *The Game of Life and How to Play It.* The rhyme of *way* and *pay* helps me remember my intention, so I can repeat it often. The phrase *wonderful service* engages my wish to offer support and hope to others. And, of course, I am open to a positive payoff in whatever form it may appear!

To manifest my goal, I have also been practicing *visualization*—a mental programming technique using vivid images. Many successful athletes use this technique to enhance their performance, among them Jordan Spieth, the youngest winner of the 2017 British Open Golf Tournament, who often refers to *seeing the shot* before he hits the ball.

As I've been writing, I often visualize a future book-signing event where people tell me how much my book has helped them. To enhance the power of my visualization, I've created two *vision boards*, portraying in pictures, colors, and words the positive experiences I will have when I reach my goal.

Figure 4.1 shows my two five-by-seven-inch, laminated vision boards. The words "Create something good. Yes, you! You're done," give me inspiration. The dove, hearts, and word *serenity* remind me of my positive power's help. The woman leaping over the round object represents me overcoming my worries and achieving my goal. Oprah Winfrey is a symbol of courage and service to others.

My vision boards are on my desk in my direct line of vision. Before I begin writing, I say my affirmations aloud, visualize them as true, and then connect my heart with the images on my boards.

Figure 4.1 Gigi's Vision Boards

To create your own vision board, cut words and illustrations from magazines, draw pictures, or use photos. Arrange them in a way that is meaningful to you on a small card or larger piece of cardboard. The only absolute is that your board portray how your life will look after meeting your goal.

Time for Action!
Tool 16. Your Affirmation

Think of a challenging situation that's been worrying you, and imagine how you would like to feel and act in that situation. Just remember, if your goal involves another person, make sure you indicate how *you* want to be rather than focusing on how you want *them* to be.

1. Use the guidelines to write your affirmation in your journal. If you'd like, add the words, "Thank you, (*the name you use for positive power*) for (*fill in the blank*)."
2. Copy your affirmation onto a sticky note, and put it in a spot where you'll frequently see it.
3. Place another copy of your intention in a small box or special place.
4. Repeat your affirmation as often as you can.
5. Make a vision board that represents how you want your life to be when your desire is accomplished.
6. Focus on your vision board images a couple of times a day and just before bedtime.
7. When you state your affirmation or look at your vision board, immerse yourself in the emotions and sensations you would have if your wish were already fulfilled.

Now that you've chosen your goal, you come face-to-face with the hardest part of the process—to let the outcome go. Your first inclination might be to try to exert control to get the exact results you want. Your best option, however, is to do the opposite: Let go by cultivating the Buddhist virtue of *nonattachment*.

Choice 2.
Let Go of Attachment

After being asked how he remained so calm in the middle of life's storms, an enlightened master replied, "I don't mind what happens." This is non-attachment. It boils down to a humble admission that your thoughts and actions, especially when they're based on worry, don't always lead to the best results. It's trusting that a power wiser than your own intellect might have a better outcome. You can then approach life without fighting it, judging it, or needing to control it.

So, if this is nonattachment, what then is *attachment?* Attachment is the mother of all worries. When you're attached, your whispered lies insist you know exactly how things should turn out. Further, you've made your own happiness dependent upon reaching a specific result.

Nonattachment offers you peaceful acceptance and creative freedom. Recall the guideline suggesting your affirmation include "in the best way for all concerned." These words signify you trust your positive power to fashion a good result, even if it looks different from your initial goal.

How do you know if you're overly attached to something? Just ask yourself, "How often do the words *should, must,* or *ought* go through my mind?" Attachment sounds like this:

- My daughter *should* stop using drugs.
- This person, (*fill in the blank*), *must* be nicer to me.
- The mayor (or president, legislator, etc.) is wrong and *ought* to (*fill in the blank*).
- I *should* be healthy and happy and never experience troubling situations.

These are examples of what Fred Luskin, the director of the Stanford University Forgiveness Project, calls *unenforceable rules.* Such rules demand an outcome you believe must come true, but over which you have no control. Luskin writes in *Forgive for Good* that these inflexible beliefs make you feel helpless, angry, hurt, hopeless or bitter.

Although holding an unenforceable rule may feel good—even noble—it doesn't mean you can make it happen. In the first example, the daughter *should* stop using drugs, but no matter how persuasive the mother's arguments, she doesn't have the power to make her daughter stop. The mother does, however, have control over her own choices and behavior. She can seek help from a therapist or Al-Anon, and claim a positive power to work in the situation. Then she might choose a goal for how she wants to act and feel, detach from the result, and use growth tools for her own peace of mind, regardless of her daughter's choices.

One of my own unenforceable rules became clear as I was writing this book. When my mother passed away, I found it difficult to write and became discouraged by my lack of progress. When I honestly faced the belief that I must complete the book by a certain date, I became willing to see it differently. After using Tool 6, Is It True? I turned my whispered lie around to "I will finish writing the book at the perfect time." In turn, I became more flexible and kinder with myself.

The essence of nonattachment is peacefully allowing life to unfold. Nothing becomes a live-or-die situation because you know your loving power is working things out, with results that may far surpass your greatest hopes.

Time for Action!
Tool 17. Detaching from Outcomes

After setting an intention, your subsequent thoughts and actions will indicate if you're overly attached to it or not. Think back to the situation and goal you considered in the last exercise (tool 16).

1. List the frequent thoughts you've had about the situation, and the actions you've taken to make it better.
2. Next to each thought or action, write A for attachment or N for nonattachment.
   Write A if your thought or action was driven by:
   • Worrying about the results;
   • Focusing on the hurtful details;

- Needing to fix your situation right away; or
- Insisting on one right solution.

Write N if your thought or action helped you:

- Focus on your own responsibilities, thoughts, and feelings;
- Affirm a positive power working toward the best for all concerned;
- Practice patience and compassion with yourself and others; or
- Listen with care and express your feelings and needs kindly.

3. Make note of the unenforceable rules or whispered lies blocking your progress.
4. Accept that it may take time for your situation to work out. Trust that using growth tools—along with honesty, positive power, and good choices—will improve your circumstances.

Now that you've released your attachment to a desired outcome, you're ready to start working toward making it a reality. Ironically, you won't begin with direct actions to reach your goal. Instead, you'll use various tools to enlist the power to achieve it.

Choice 3.
Get to Work

Growth practices flow loving power into your mind, spirit, and body energy. With fewer whispered lies blocking your life force, you're more open to insights and actions that lead unerringly toward a happy and peaceful future.

Take a moment to review the previous seventeen tools. If you've already tried some of them, congratulations on starting to overcome your worries and fears. Were you surprised that using any of these practices once or twice didn't completely silence your whispered lies? Rest assured that it takes continuous practice to reprogram the negative thoughts and beliefs that have run your life for so long.

Here's where your willpower comes in handy. Instead of using it to meet your goal, apply your willpower to regularly using worry-dissolving practices. A good place to start is with a daily quiet time.

Tool 18. Daily Quiet Time

When I take time to connect with my positive power at the beginning of the day, good things happen. On most mornings, I spend five to twenty minutes in my favorite chair as I drink my coffee. Since I'm barely awake and my mind hasn't started racing, it's a great time to fill it with inspiration and courage.

I often begin by noticing the play of sunlight, shadows, and colors in my living room, or the antics of Murphy, my cat. I usually ponder an inspirational reading. Sometimes I write in my journal, and I always say one or more prayers. When I'm finished, I'm ready to "play ball" in the game of life.

Why is it so important to have a daily quiet time? The practices weave a safety net that catches you when life brings an unexpected challenge. When you start the day with a tightly woven net of peace and strength, you can handle these challenges with patience and grace.

Sometimes you'll let up on your daily practices, as we all do on occasion, and your safety net slowly frays. You may notice a humming tension in your body or the incessant chatter of whispered lies. When a difficulty arises, you find you have little wisdom, patience, or resilience. You might bark at a loved one or curl up in a ball of despair. During such times, immediately begin reweaving your safety net by using one or two of your favorite tools. Soon you'll find your serenity and hope restored.

One of my favorite growth practices is loving-kindness. Take a moment to experience its transformative power.

Time for Action!
Tool 19. Loving-Kindness Practice

The loving-kindness practice Buddhists call *metta* calms your mind, opens your heart to goodness and care, and helps you claim the power of your true self. The practice also asks for the healing of your fears, worries, and whispered lies so you can serve others' growth.

1. Read the following words aloud, pause, and then read them again.
   May I be at peace. May my heart remain open.
   May I awaken to the light of my own true nature.
   May I be healed. May I be a source of healing for all beings.
2. With one or more of your loved ones in mind, say the prayer again changing *I* to *you: May you be at peace. May your heart . . .*
3. Next, change *you* to *we: May we be at peace . . .*
4. Now use the *May you* version of the prayer for a person you feel is causing you worry, frustration, or pain. Whenever you have a negative thought about this person, repeat the phrases of loving-kindness and notice how you begin to respond differently.

Loving-kindness widens the influence of positive power in the world. As you connect with the light of your own true nature, you'll find you can't afford to hold mean-spirited thoughts about another person or group.

Claiming loving-kindness is one way to set a positive intention for your day—an important aspect of daily practice. As you look forward to the day, envision how you want to be with the people you'll encounter. You might choose to be peaceful, kind, patient, compassionate, joyful, courageous, competent, or some other way. Affirm your desire out loud or in writing, and then release your attachment to it. Have compassion for yourself if you falter, and then use your favorite growth tools to get back on track. You'll find your day unfolding in surprisingly positive directions.

People who regularly take time to connect with their loving power receive a mysterious benefit: *meaningful coincidences.* Some say a coincidence is positive power's way of remaining anonymous. Regardless of how they occur, such unexpected events produce new possibilities.

Just the Right Next Practice

After I set the goal to write this book, I experienced a period of turmoil and resistance I call the *backlash effect.* My whispered lies seemed to wake up and say, "What? This can't be! There's no way you're going do *that!*" "You can't get this honest about your life; people will think you're neurotic," and "You can't handle it if people criticize you." Suddenly, I found myself unable to write.

A quote from W. H. Murray sums up the coincidences I experienced soon after I hit that block: "The moment one definitely commits oneself, then providence moves too. All sorts of things occur to help one that would never otherwise have occurred."

Despite knowing about the many benefits of meditation, I had never been able to get the hang of it. I just couldn't quiet my incessant thinking long enough to feel successful. Then providence moved in a surprising way.

- While at lunch with my friend Chris, who had just completed her first book, I shared my fears about my writing. She told me how meditating had calmed her mind and given her a connection to a source of wise guidance in her work.
- Soon after, I made a new friend, Mara, who meditates for twenty minutes twice a day. I became envious of her unflappable sense of peace.
- Later that month, a woman in my book club mentioned she recently began meditating as part of her treatment for shingles and had not had an episode since.
- After spontaneously deciding to attend a women's retreat, I found when I arrived that the topic was meditation! As the weekend progressed, I began to believe I could actually integrate this practice into my life.
- A few days after the retreat, a friend asked me to join her for Deepak Chopra and Oprah Winfrey's twenty-one-day online meditation challenge.

At that point, I looked up to the heavens, and said, "OK, OK!" and began to meditate most mornings.

I find if I skip my morning meditation, I have less serenity and cour-age to handle life's challenges. Recently, I began the day by reading many emails about a retreat I was leading. When I later went to my desk to piece together some new ideas for this chapter, I noticed I was tense and couldn't find the right words. I stopped, asked myself, "What's wrong?" and remembered I had neglected to meditate.

Instead of criticizing myself, I gave myself kudos for noticing my ten-sion. Recalling that it's never too late to start a day over, I did just that. As I entered the stillness, I could almost hear my body saying, "OK, the wise one is driving the bus now. We can stop the high alert." I received a wondrous result: I wrote the exact words I had been searching for ear-lier. I was no longer stuck!

If you want more energy, peace, and productivity, try establishing a regular meditation practice.

Time for Action!
Tool 20. Meditation

Did you know meditation is equally as effective in treating some forms of anxiety and depression as antidepressant medi-cation? Madhav Goyal, professor of medicine at Johns Hopkins, reviewed forty-seven studies that support this finding. If you, like many of us, have difficulty quieting your busy thoughts, try some guided meditations.

1. Set your alarm to wake you twenty to thirty minutes earlier than usual.
2. Use Insight Timer (free app), the web, or YouTube to access a meditation topic that might be helpful for you, perhaps courage, calmness, or forgiveness. Or choose to meditate with silence or music.
3. Meditate for fifteen to twenty minutes each day for a week.

After meditating, notice how you feel about some of the situations that had been worrying you. You'll be amazed, as I was, how it melts away your fears.

Energy Psychology

While having coffee with a work associate, I mentioned I had started work on this book. She exclaimed, "You've got to meet my aunt. She just wrote a book, and she's amazing!" My friend's aunt, Joan Feldman, is an author and social worker full of vitality, enthusiasm, and love. In *A Frog in My Basement: A Therapist's Curious Journey into Energy Psychology and the Law of Attraction*, Joan describes how she moved from using traditional talk therapy to less conventional energy techniques. Her book is honest, witty, and helpful—everything I hope my book turns out to be.

When I explained how my worries were getting in the way of my work, Joan assured me my fears were normal. In only three sessions, she taught me a quick and easy energy practice to overcome my whispered lies. And, to my amazement, I was then able to resume working.

Emotional Freedom Technique (EFT) is a form of energy psychology created by Stanford engineer, Gary Craig. It's often referred to as *tapping therapy*. Joan began by having me identify a thought that made me feel upset. I chose, "I'll never be able to handle public criticism of my book." As we talked, I realized this was an echo of my father's chastising words when I made mistakes.

Joan then had me tap several times on my hands, chest, and face while I repeated aloud, "Even though I may face criticism of my book, and it may feel like Dad telling me I'm dumb, I love and accept myself completely." Before and after each round of tapping, Joan asked me to rate my level of distress on a scale of one to ten. She had me repeat the tapping routine until the rating went down to almost zero, which took about five times.

After Joan's sessions, I found that, although I could recall the content of my fears, I couldn't recreate the strong emotions I had felt before. Experts believe the tapping temporarily deactivates the emotional response the brain expects to have to the negative phrase. It essentially dissolved my negativity by rewiring my neural pathways.

Whenever I'm pinned down by fears and worries, I use a version of tapping called Whole Health: Easily and Effectively (WHEE), developed by Daniel J. Benor. I highly recommend his book, *Seven Minutes to Natural Pain Release.* In this approach, there is no need to memorize a series of tapping points. You simply alternate tapping on two sides of the body. For instance, you can cross your arms and tap on the sides of your upper arms, or put your palms on the sides of your thighs and alternate tapping there.

When I use tapping, I usually add a statement of reassurance from my positive power. Here are a few examples:

- "Even though I'm stuck and I'm afraid I'll never finish my book, I love and accept myself completely, and *positive power loves and accepts me unconditionally.*"
- "Even though my flaws may be out in the open, I love and accept myself completely, *as does my loving power.*"
- "Even though it's taking a long time to revise this book, I am lovable and acceptable, and *God knows it, too.*"

After using this energy technique, I've left each session feeling lighter and more relaxed.

Time for Action!
Tool 21. Tapping Therapy

Do you have doubts about the scientific base for energy techniques? You may want to check out Fred P. Gallo's *Energy Tapping* and David Feinstein's *The Promise of Energy Psychology* to confirm the effectiveness of tapping in treating depression, anxiety, trauma, pain, and stress. The only way to know if it will work for you is to try it.

1. Go to a website such as eftzone.com, eftuniverse.com, or danielbenor.com to learn a tapping strategy. Even better, have a coach or therapist guide you through the process a few times. I recommend the latter if you've had trauma of any kind and not resolved it with a therapist.

2. Select one painful event or belief you think is keeping you stuck.

3. Before tapping, think about the event or belief, and rate your level of emotional or physical intensity on a scale of one to ten.

4. Create a statement of your exact fear followed by a reassuring phrase: "Even though I feel (*add detail about the fears*), I love and accept myself completely." If you wish, add "and my (*the name you use for positive power*) loves and accepts me completely."

5. Keep tapping while repeating two or three times both the statement and the reassuring phrases.

6. Afterward, rate your emotional intensity on a scale of one to ten.

7. If your intensity rating is not significantly lower, try another few cycles, or engage a coach or therapist.

Although these techniques helped me overcome my writing blocks, I had even more challenges to face. A month before the planned publication date, I was quite anxious about my decision to subcontract with six different professionals for editing, typesetting, proofreading, book cover design, marketing, and printing. My mind whispered, "It won't be good enough to help others," and "It won't get done on time."

I used one of my favorite tools for overcoming my fear: Tool 22. It helped me relax, practice nonattachment, and allow the publishing process to move along its appointed path. Perhaps you'll find it helpful, too.

Time for Action!
Tool 22. The Activity of God Affirmation

This affirmation expresses the premise of this book: *Positive power can and will dissolve your whispered lies.* As you repeat the words of Unity School of Christianity minister, J. Sig Paulson, feel free to use the name of your positive power instead of God.

1. Read this silently:

   > *The activity of God is the only power at work*
   > *in my mind, heart, and life.*
   > *All false beliefs, all negative appearances are dissolved*
   > *right now by the loving, forgiving action of God.*
   > *I am whole, strong, and free as God created me to be.*

2. Ponder the meaning of the first part: *The activity of God is the only power at work in my mind, heart, and life.* Here you assert your positive power is supreme, stronger than your past wounds, greater than your worries, and wiser than your intellect. This benevolent power is the only one you want to influence your life.

3. Consider the second sentence: *All false beliefs, all negative appearances are dissolved right now by the loving, forgiving action of God.* Your loving power dissolves your limiting beliefs and washes away your sludge-like fears, creating space for goodness and wisdom to enter your life. The word forgiveness doesn't refer to sin or any other dogma. It simply means releasing the negative thoughts and actions that separate you from your goodness.

4. In the last sentence, *I am whole, strong, and free as God created me to be,* you assert the truth of who you are; not the person you may present to the world, but your true self, endowed with positive power.

5. Whenever you have a negative thought or feeling, repeat the Activity of God Affirmation. Then look for the moment when your fears suddenly shrink, replaced by love, inspiration, hope, and joy.

These words remind me that my whispered lies are making my problems appear more difficult than they are, and these appearances are merely figments of my overactive imagination. My fears subside as I affirm the protective benefit of loving power.

Using affirmations and visualization, detaching from judgments about the quality and pace of my work, and consistently applying several growth practices helped fulfill my dream to write this book.

Perhaps you have your own dream you'd like to pursue. As you continue making positive choices, you'll uncover a powerful source of intuitive guidance and strength—your true self.

Summary

- What you focus your mind upon determines your future.
- When setting goals, cultivate nonattachment and the willingness to have your wishes manifest in unexpected ways.
- Consistently use growth practices to focus on power and goodness rather than fear and worry.
- Meditation, affirmations, and tapping are powerful tools for manifesting your desires.

Chapter 5

Using Growth Practices to Recover Your True Self
Strategy Four

You do not become good by trying to be good,
but by finding the goodness that is already within you
and allowing that goodness to emerge.
—Eckhart Tolle, A New Earth: Awakening
to Your Life's Purpose

How connected are you with your *true self*, the *you* that lies in your heart, not your head? Your true self is unfettered by old wounds; it's courageous, generous, and powerful enough to fulfill your dreams. Too often, however, these assets lie buried under the damage left by a critical parent, competitive sibling, mean-spirited teacher, abusive relative, debilitating illness, or dysfunctional family.

Such experiences contribute to what Swiss psychiatrist Carl Jung called the *shadow-self*. This unconscious negativity is the author of your deepest worries and false beliefs. Jung and most experts agree that denying the existence of your shadow increases its damaging effects on your life.

The good news is the strongest and most valuable aspects of your personality have never left you; they are only temporarily hidden by your shadow's fear and pain. As you honestly face your whispered lies, claim positive power, choose a desired future, and use growth practices, you clear the way to express your true self in the world.

Here you'll see how I healed several layers of my shadow by facing my most secret and debilitating childhood experience. As I used growth tools to overcome my hidden pain and fears, I gained a new outlook on life—one of hope, love, and peace.

A New Pair of Glasses

Because our minds naturally focus on worry's whispered lies, we need growth practices to help us see people and situations from a *new perspective*. Think of it as putting on a new pair of glasses. Without them, all you see is an intimidating and threatening world. With your glasses on, though, you see a peaceful place beyond your whispered lies.

When you're facing confusion, conflict, or other troubles, begin by honestly admitting that your perception is distorted by the fearful aspects of your issue. Ask your positive power to change your point of view, perhaps by saying that you reject your false beliefs and want to see things differently.

Rumi, the thirteenth-century Persian poet and Sufi mystic, wrote, "Out beyond ideas of wrongdoing and rightdoing is a field. I will meet you there." Figure 5.1 illustrates how looking "beyond the contours" of your fears leads you to a field where a new perspective lies.

It's a choice between *living in the problem* and *living in the solution.*

- *Living in the problem (Fear).* The jagged edges of our worries capture our attention and confine it to our problem's details. We imagine who was at fault, what we should have said or done, or how a situation should be different. These fears make us tense and unhappy.
- *Living in the solution (Love).* When negative thoughts come to mind, we acknowledge them, reject them, and use growth practices to refocus our thoughts on where the solution lies— our loving power. Soon, we gain a new perspective, leading to positive feelings and actions.

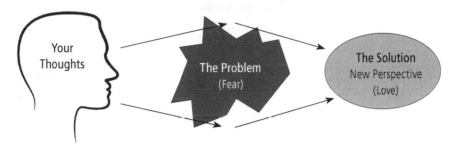

Figure 5.1. Looking Beyond Fear to a New Perspective

So, when you're captured—enthralled even—by a tangle of negative feelings, how can you tap into love's solutions? In the early twentieth century, Emmet Fox, a leader of the New Thought Movement, developed the Golden Key—one of the most effective tools in this book.

The Golden Key turns your thoughts away from the problem and toward positive power. Fox wrote the persistent use of it resolves situations in the most amazing ways. I agree, as I've seen wonderful results in my own and in others' lives.

Recently, I argued with my husband by insisting the GPS was giving us the wrong directions. My fearful mind whispered that he must admit I was right. I then stopped and asked my positive power to help me see this differently. I took a few deep breaths, and silently repeated the Serenity Prayer. Suddenly, my inner voice gently asked, "Would you rather be right or would you rather be at peace?" As I chose peace, the heat of my emotions dissolved. Later, my husband and I had a good laugh when we saw that my "better" route was different—but no shorter than—the GPS's route!

Time for Action!
Tool 23. The Golden Key

I invite you to try the Golden Key for the next two days. You'll be pleasantly surprised.

1. Select a troubling situation in your life and write a few sentences about it in your journal.
2. Rate the level of your emotional disturbance on a scale of one to ten, one being the least intense and ten being the most intense.
3. Choose a phrase or image to use when you catch yourself worrying: an affirmation (all is well), a word (peace), a prayer (thank you for helping me see this differently), or a characteristic of loving power (wisdom). You might focus on an image of beauty (a pristine lake, a rose) or write a gratitude list. If you're Catholic, you could recite the rosary.
4. Select a method to remind yourself to check your thoughts several times each day. You may want to put a string on your wrist, and when you notice it, ask yourself what you're thinking or feeling at that moment. Perhaps you'll set a timer to go off every one or two hours; when it rings, ask yourself the same question. Or post a sticky note in a prominent spot as a reminder.
5. Your mind is well trained to be worried. When you notice it returning to your problem, gently resume thinking about your phrase or image. No matter how frequently you need to redirect your mind, the process will work if you stick with it.
6. At the end of each day, describe in your journal how your situation appears to you, rate your level of emotional disturbance, and compare it to your earlier rating.

Your new perspective may come quickly or slowly, but it will come. You'll notice a sense of lightness and freedom, and find it hard to recapture the heat of the old fear-based feelings. This peaceful outlook will help you know exactly what to do; or you may realize no action is necessary.

Every time I've started healing a new piece of my shadow, the Golden Key, along with other growth tools, has helped me look beyond the contours of my troubles to the field of love and its solutions.

Is It Really in Perfect Order?

The following quote (some attribute it to Buddha) is one of my favorites: "When you realize how perfect everything is, you will tilt your head back and laugh at the sky."

When parts of your shadow begin to emerge, it's especially important to trust the principle of *perfect order*. Sometimes you'll think you can't possibly handle another disturbing piece of your past. At other times, you'll think you're making no headway. If you stay in touch with your positive power, however, you'll ultimately see the beautiful orchestration of your progress.

When I first got sober, I couldn't bear to look at my past, fearing the pain would erupt in a blast, flatten me, and I'd never be able to get up. Folksinger Iris DeMent perfectly expressed my dread in a song about her father's death, "No Time to Cry": "And if the feelings start to comin', I've learned to stop 'em fast. 'Cause I don't know, if I let 'em go, they might not wanna pass."

I'm glad to report that this never happened. My experience was similar to learning how to lift weights from an experienced trainer. If you've never lifted, he might have you start with five pounds. After a few weeks, he'll slowly increase the weight, giving you eight pounds. At first, you might doubt you're strong enough, but your trainer reassures you, and you soon find yourself lifting progressively heavier weights with ease. Eventually, you reach your goal: You're lifting a fifteen-pound weight.

Your loving power is like a trainer who allows a part of your shadow to surface only when you have the strength to face it. Figure 5.2 illustrates three stages of my own growth. As each layer appeared, I feared I wouldn't be able to handle it, but the Four Strategies and tools gave me safe passage.

When I first glimpsed a negative aspect of my personality, I often went through a period of shock, alternating between denying my shadow-self and claiming the power to face it. The arrows pointing back and forth between each of the Four Strategies represent moments—sometimes days or weeks—when I wavered between letting fear stop me and

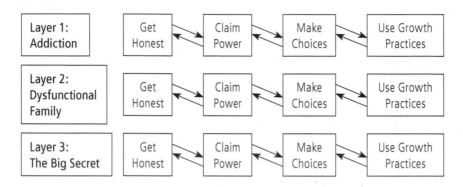

Figure 5.2. The Four Strategies Heal Multiple Layers

moving forward. Because I was making healthy choices and consistently using growth practices, I overcame those blocks.

At the end of each layer of healing, I recovered a valuable piece of my true self. I was stronger, happier, and more peaceful. After a period of enjoying these rewards, a new layer would appear and the process would continue.

Layer 1: Addiction

Chapters 2–4 described how I got *honest* about my alcohol and drug abuse. My Twelve-Step meetings helped me find a *power* that could improve my life. Next, I *chose* to have a healthy future and committed to do the work to get there: I consistently used the *practices* of connecting with growth partners, as well as prayer, gratitude lists, affirmations, meditation, and therapy.

Only small parts of my shadow emerged at first. For instance, I challenged the whispered lie that, without a man to love me, I was worthless. For many years, this lie had fostered my pattern of using romantic relationships as a source of self-worth.

To gain a more reliable sense of myself, I reprogrammed my mind with verbal affirmations such as, "I am lovable," and "There is nothing to fear; my worth is established by positive power." Whenever I obsessed about wanting a man in my life, I gave myself loving messages. My friendships with healthy women—who accepted me exactly as I was—taught me I didn't need a man's attention to feel good about myself.

All this footwork kept me on the right track. I had caring friends, had stopped using alcohol and drugs, and was letting go of seeking security through romance.

Layer 2: Dysfunctional Family

After eight months of sobriety, my Twelve-Step sponsor suggested I take a personal inventory of my fears, resentments, and harmful sexual behavior. Soon after, I shared these embarrassing facts with her. Amazingly, she didn't seem shocked by my past. Admitting to another person the secrets I had kept hidden for so long gave me great relief.

My first inventory revealed I was a perfectionist and had a great fear of making mistakes. To overcome the lie that I couldn't be loved unless I was perfect, I continued therapy, positive affirmations, the Golden Key, and my morning quiet time.

When I was ready, my therapist and I began to explore my family of origin. I was the fourth child of a charming, alcoholic father and a mother who spent her life worrying about him. Many evenings we'd find Mom lying alone on her bed reading a book, gloomy and sad as she listened for the crunch of Dad's car tires on the driveway. Too often, that sound never came and she sank lower and lower into her sadness.

Partying with friends was the mainstay of my parents' lives. The stereo got louder and louder as the drinks got stronger and stronger. Some nights, after the guests had left, we were awakened by crashes and Mom's screams. I lay frozen in my bed as the whispered lie "I'll never be safe" sank into my bones.

When I shared these incidents, my therapist suggested I attend Twelve-Step meetings for adult children of alcoholics. Although it was uncomfortable listening to others talk about experiences similar to mine, I also felt a giddy sense of relief. I realized I wasn't alone; and if others had the courage to recover, so could I.

In alcoholic and other dysfunctional families, the dominant messages are: Don't feel, don't trust, and don't tell anyone about it. The "it" is the proverbial "elephant in the room"; although everyone is aware of it, they quickly deny it.

In the absence of honest communication about my dad's drinking, we children began to invent stories to explain the swirling tension in the air. I birthed a new whispered lie: "I must be a bad person if my parents won't give me time or attention."

Family alcoholism isn't the only condition that can stunt a child's sense of security and worth. Any trauma that causes ongoing despair can become the elephant in the room: death of a family member, physical impairment, mental illness, gambling, drug addiction, violence, chronic illness, foster care, sexual abuse, or neglect. In such cases, the troubling situations consume the family's attention, and the emotional needs of the children often go unmet. These deficits launch the child on a lifelong search for love and safety without a road map.

Adult children of alcoholics and trauma victims tend to share several characteristics. Janet G. Woititz's *Adult Children of Alcoholics* and Tian Dayton's *The ACoA Trauma Syndrome: The Impact of Childhood Pain on Adult Relationships* explain that these people often:

- Fear losing control; are overly responsible; have trouble relaxing and having fun;
- Fear their emotions or feelings; confuse pity with love; have difficulties with intimacy;
- Fear abandonment; constantly seek approval;
- Self-criticize; have low self-esteem;
- Deny reality; avoid conflict; adopt a victim mentality; become comfortable living in chaos and drama;
- Overreact to outside changes; when afraid, see everything and everyone in extremes;
- Adopt compulsive behaviors; have an attraction to compulsive personalities; and
- Suffer from frequent physical illness and an accumulation of grief.

When I first learned about these tendencies, I felt hopeless. Then I heard these empowering words: *I am not to blame for what happened to me as a child; but I am responsible for healing my past.*

As I continued to work with my therapist, I discovered that I still felt, deep inside, like a defenseless little girl. In an inner-child healing exercise, I visualized locking my mind's critical voices in a lead-lined vault. I then greeted my imaginary little girl with love and asked if she would talk with me. As my therapist coached me, I told my inner child I loved her and praised her for being so brave in our crazy home. I thanked her for inventing strategies to keep us secure, and explained that she could let go of her perfectionism and other defenses. Finally, I assured her that she could trust me—her adult self, powered by love—to keep us safe and happy.

These exercises helped me see my divorces and addictions as merely misguided attempts to find love and security. I let go of my self-condemnation and began to believe I could be happy.

Time for Action!
Tool 24. Substituting Truth Phrases for Whispered Lies

Subconscious whispered lies are the instigators of your most fearful emotions. You'll need to identify these lies clearly before you can change them. The following exercise draws on cognitive therapy and brain science to reprogram your negative thoughts.

1. In your journal, write or draw pictures about a troubling life situation. Send your inner censor away, and put whatever you feel or think on the paper. To access your most vulnerable self, try using your nondominant hand.
2. List the feelings you had as you drew or wrote. You might have felt angry, insulted, disappointed, guilty, distrustful, helpless, alone, envious, dominated, afraid, hurt, wronged, sad, pessimistic, or other feelings.
3. Discuss these with someone you trust—a growth partner, religious advisor, or counselor.

Whispered Lies (Fearful Mind)	Truth Phrases (Loving Mind)
Fears 1. I don't fit in. I'm alone. 2. I'm too weak to handle life. 3. No one really loves me.	**Truths** 1. Positive power comforts me. 2. I receive the wisdom to handle life. 3. I attract healthy loving people into my life.
Resentments 1. Life shouldn't be so hard. 2. They are too cruel, selfish, etc.	**Acceptance** 1. My life is in perfect order. 2. They are fear-filled humans, as am I.
Limiting Beliefs 1. I am not good enough. 2. They should respect and love me. 3. They should help me. 4. Nothing ever changes. I'm stuck.	**New Beliefs** 1. My essence is perfect right now. 2. I love and appreciate myself, no matter what is going on. 3. My true self knows how to handle this. 4. Positive power works miracles in my life.
Negative Attitudes 1. I hate this. 2. I hate my life.	**Positive Attitudes** 1. It's OK. Good will come out of this. 2. I'm willing to change; I appreciate my life.
False Perceptions 1. It's not fair. 2. I'm trapped.	**New Perceptions** 1. These hard experiences help me grow. 2. I'm free of my past patterns.
Guilt and Shame 1. I should know better. 2. I'm a loser.	**Trusting Love** 1. My loving power knows everything I need to know at this time. 2. As I trust positive power, I receive everything I need.

Figure 5.3. Whispered Lies and Truth Phrases

4. On the left side of figure 5.3, circle the whispered lies underlying your turmoil. Add other false beliefs you might discover.

5. In your journal, list the whispered lies you want to leave behind.
6. Alongside each of them, write the associated truth phrase from the right side of the figure (or create your own).
7. Whenever you're anxious about a situation, identify your false belief and say the relevant truth phrases.
8. Monitor your negative self-talk, and repeat step 7 as often as necessary.
9. Check your list of whispered lies and truth phrases each week, and revise them as needed. Note any changes in your thinking or feelings about your situation.

In a matter of minutes, hours, or days, your responses to the world will be less defensive, judgmental, self-centered, or dramatic. Your troubling situations will seem easier to handle, if they haven't already improved significantly.

Layer 3: The Big Secret

After a few more years, a secret that lay deep in my shadow surfaced.

One day, I told a friend that I had just seen a TV program about date rape and was so grateful nothing like it had ever happened to me. At that exact moment, I felt a queasy lurch in my stomach as I realized something like that *had* happened to me.

After the initial shock wore off, it occurred to me that, with all the chaos in our home, who knew what might have occurred? The next day, I found a new therapist who specialized in sexual abuse. After a few sessions, Sharon asked me to recall the first time a sexual boundary had been crossed.

At first, I couldn't remember anything (denial is difficult to crack!), but later that week I wrote this poem:

> *I've asked Dad to awaken me*
> *To go riding in the misty dawn,*
> *As I slowly rise to the surface,*
> *His touch comes out of the fog.*

"Was that a hand on my breast?"
But he's already gone.

This memory opened a deep well of dark and scary feelings. Although I was determined to heal, I wasn't sure I could do it. Once again, I stepped up my growth practices to access love's healing power, and was soon led to just the right resources.

Laura Davis's *The Courage to Heal* suggests that, since memories of sexual abuse are often clothed in mystery, it isn't necessary to uncover every detail or instance. Instead of worrying about the exact form of my abuse, my focus needed to be accepting—and then healing—my emotions.

Those facing past abuse or neglect will find it important to treat themselves with respect, loving care, and kindness. The following tools gave me the support I needed as I made my journey toward healing. If you've had similar problems, I hope you'll benefit from my experience as you recover your true self.

Tool 25. Self-Nurturing

After each therapy session, I took time to tend to my raw feelings. Instead of scheduling work appointments, I nurtured myself by taking a nap, writing in my journal, or going to the gym. On several afternoons, I just lay in my bed, cried, and rested. These self-soothing actions were a balm to my fragile state and gave me the strength to continue.

Tool 26. Group Therapy

Sharon eventually suggested I join the weekly therapy group she led. As uncomfortable as it was to share my experiences, the other women's honesty and courage helped me face my past.

Later that year, something my sister said set off an alarm in my mind. When she complained about how Dad "copped a feel" whenever he hugged her, I suddenly realized that he did the same to me.

The next time Sharon's group met, I described in detail how my father hugged me by placing his palms on my rib cage and rubbing his thumbs on the sides of my breasts. When I told the women he was still hugging me in this way, their shocked silence—followed by outraged responses—broke through my remaining denial.

Tool 27. Writing an Unsent Letter

Although I had long avoided negative feelings toward my parents, it was time to acknowledge and express them in a healthy way. Sharon suggested I write about my anger, sadness, and hurt in a letter I would never send. As I wrote, I poured out my rage about how my father's sexual touching had set me up for a series of failed relationships, promiscuity, and addictions. I expressed my fury that my mother had not protected me. After sharing the letter with Sharon, I burned it, along with the scars it represented—a liberating action.

Tool 28. Setting Boundaries

Sharon soon asked if I was ready to tell my father how I wanted him to hug me in the future. By asserting and enforcing this *boundary*, I could reclaim the power to keep myself safe.

I wrote a short letter asking him if we could talk one-on-one during my Thanksgiving visit. Before leaving, I rehearsed the words I would use and prayed for the courage to say what I needed to say. Shortly after I arrived, Dad and I went into a den where I made sure the door remained open. After saying a silent prayer, I repeated my memorized script: "Dad, when you hug me and put your thumbs on the sides of my breasts, it makes me very uncomfortable. I want you to stop doing that."

I held my breath, waiting for his response. He said simply, "Oh, OK. I didn't know that." I was amazed—no defensiveness, no apologies, just those few words. We went back to the living room as if nothing had happened. I was exhausted. My father never hugged me in that disturbing way again.

Setting that boundary was one of the most frightening and valuable things I had ever done. It destroyed the whispered lie that I was a victim who couldn't protect herself; and it taught me I was a strong and courageous woman.

My new assertiveness carried over into my work life when I accepted extra responsibility for a high-level committee. Before then, I would have sacrificed those additional ten hours a week without remuneration. Empowered by my newfound strength, I asked for, and received compensatory time.

Tool 29. Energy Healing

Even after so much growth, I often felt tense and anxious. Deep down, I feared that I had invited my father's sexual touching—enjoyed it even. This concern spawned a new whispered lie: "This happened because I'm a bad person." When I got honest about my shame, I received help from a surprising source.

For months, I had been hearing about the power of energy healing. I saw an article about it in a magazine and noticed several people talking about it. Then a friend told me about her wonderful experience with an energy healing practitioner. Trusting the synchronicity of these events, I immediately made an appointment.

After listening to my history, Carol explained that a form of energy work called "cranial-sacral therapy" could release the shame locked in my body. After the first session, I noticed only a slightly fizzy feeling in my extremities. But the second session transformed me.

As I lay on my back, Carol placed her palms lightly on the sides of my head, and asked me to cross my hands and feet and say, "All parts of me are innocent, pure, and sinless." As I repeated this phrase, I was hoping for a dramatic response. Nothing happened. When I asked my positive power to help me believe the words, my shame suddenly evaporated.

At the end of the session, Carol said, "As you live each moment, your job is to claim that all parts of you are pure and sinless." I left her office feeling free and whole. I was relieved that the shame was just an illusion; it had nothing to do with my true self.

Now that you've seen how the most painful wounds can heal in perfect order, it's time to get to work.

Time for Action!
Your Own Growth Program

How has your past kept you stuck in old patterns of thinking or behaving? How would your life change if you could replace your worries and fears with love, confidence, and courage? You can reach your dreams by committing to your own program of growth.

1. Begin a daily practice, if you haven't already done so. Go back through the previous twenty-nine tools and select one or two to use every day.
2. Choose a few of your most limiting beliefs, and select two or three tools to help you find a new healthy perspective.
3. Make a commitment to use your daily practices and other growth tools for the next month.
4. Notice the changes in your situations and self-awareness.

It takes great courage to escape the bondage of your past wounds and become your best self. It certainly took more bravery than I thought I had to tell you the story of my sexual abuse. Every time I approached my writing desk, my mind cautioned, "Don't open those old wounds," and "You can't tell your family's secrets." Rather than believe those lies, I pursued therapy and energy work to dissolve their influence. And now, I offer you this completed chapter.

Although a few enlightened beings may never give in to their whispered lies, most of us struggle daily with our negative thinking. The trick is to move ahead anyway, with honesty, power, healthy choices, and growth practices.

Even with these positive actions, you will sometimes think the pace of your growth isn't fast enough.

Trust the Process

As your layers emerge and you explore them, there will be ups and downs in your healing. Sometimes things may seem to be getting worse rather than better. You might wake up filled with dread, sadness, or pain. Perhaps you'll stubbornly refuse to use any helpful tools.

Please don't give up. Trust that your process is in perfect order: It's moving at just the right pace in just the right way, even though it may not feel that way. Stick with your program as best you can, and try a few of the following tools to comfort, fortify, and inspire you.

Tool 30. Acting as If

During challenging times, my friends often suggest that I *act as if*. Even if I might not feel like it, I should act as if what I want is already in place. Pretend—yes, *pretend*—you are who you want to be, and respond as that person would. Choose to act as if everything is proceeding in just the right way.

Compel yourself to use just one growth practice, and then feel good about doing this one thing. Faking it in this way is the ultimate trust walk. Eventually, your clouds of doubt will disappear, and you'll operate from a place of strength and love.

Tool 31. The Backlash Effect

When we begin to act in new healthy ways, we often experience a *backlash*: Instead of feeling great about our new behavior, we feel ill at ease. It's as if the old, well-established neural pathways rise up in rebellion. In my experience, this discomfort is a cause for celebration.

One of my friends recently told me she was furious with her former husband because of his failure to pay child support. To let go of her anger, she'd been following the suggestion that she pray for him; but when she did, she felt awful—worse, in fact! Wasn't she supposed to be feeling more peaceful and forgiving? Why wasn't it working?

I explained that her feeling of turmoil was a backlash effect. The loving action of praying for her ex-husband had rattled the cage of the whispered lies that wanted to blame him for her unhappiness. I suggested she see her discomfort as evidence of going against the grain of her old patterns. Her uncomfortable feelings soon passed as her prayers and other growth practices gave her the courage to kindly but assertively pursue child support.

Tool 32. Progress, Not Perfection

If you suffer from perfectionism and its equally negative twin, self-condemnation, try adopting this little mantra: *Progress, not perfection.* Say it to yourself often, trusting that perfect order is at work even when your growth seems too slow.

To counteract perfectionism, write down the many ways you've already become stronger, and then make a gratitude list (tool 15).

Tool 33. Frequent Contact with Growth Partners

When you feel discouraged, it's especially important to share your frustrations with a growth partner, counselor, or therapist. Their wisdom, reassurance, and love will help you stick with your program. Most important, the trust you build with these advisors will give you hope and connection.

Tool 34. Waiting with Patience

One of the wisest sayings I've heard is: *Sometimes waiting is an action.* When I'm worried my situation will never improve, I remember that I won't feel that way forever. In the meantime, I don't do anything rash or self-destructive.

I often gain patience by observing myself from a place of detachment, as in Tool 8, The Balcony View. Usually I see that my fearful mind is causing me to "live in the wreckage of my future." Then I remind myself that, although my feelings may *seem* real, they are not necessarily based on reality. Once again, I ask my positive power for a new perspective.

Tool 35. The Basics: HALTS

When you are out of sorts, check to see if you are *Hungry, Angry, Lonely, Tired, or Sick (HALTS)*. Some people wisely add a second T for Thirsty. You may be especially subject to negative thinking under any of these conditions.

Recently, the day after a golf outing, I wrote this journal entry:

Today I tried to meditate and all I could think about were the things I didn't like—for example, my bad attitude during golf and people interfering with my plans. My attitude sucks! I should pray or make a gratitude list, but I just can't bring myself to do either one. OK, what's going on here? Let's check HALTS.

Am I Hungry? Yes, I've not eaten breakfast yet and it's already 10:30 a.m.

Am I Angry? Yes, I'm mad that the retreat planning is taking up so much of my time; that someone promised a scholarship to a woman without letting me know; that golf yesterday was no fun.

Am I Lonely? No. Well, maybe I am. During the golf event, I couldn't hear the jokes and other small talk. My hearing wasn't up to the task. So, I sat there silently and felt left out. (Make audiologist appointment today.)

Am I Tired? OK, here's the big one. I've been overdoing—again!! When I get too busy, my whispered lies grab the micro-phone and drown out all the healthy voices. I go into poor-me mode and I shouldn't trust a thought!

Am I Sick? Yes. My wrist hurts from too much gardening and too much golf; I hate pain.

This self-care inventory told me that I needed to eat breakfast, which I did immediately. Then I meditated on self-compassion, called the audi-ologist, and settled down to a nap with my kitty, Murphy. Taking these actions restored my hopeful outlook, and I had a wonderful day.

Tool 36. A Renewal Break
The hilarious and insightful author, Anne Lamott, refers to a *renewal break* as her own personal cruise vacation. It's a time where she might

spend an undisturbed afternoon on her couch with her favorite magazines. My friend, Mara, calls her renewal break "being a cat!"

I recently became disheartened while writing this chapter. My first instinct was to force its progress by ramping up my effort. But, after a few breaths to calm myself, I decided to do something pleasurable instead.

At first, my fears whispered, "You can't do that! This book will never get finished!" But in my gut—the spot that tells the truth—I knew it was the right thing to do. We were on vacation and I had only enjoyed the beach a couple of times. I gathered up my chair and a few brightly colored towels, and headed out. I wrote this in my journal when I returned:

> *For a while, I just savored the sound of the waves as I gazed at the fluffy clouds. Then a soaring seagull caught my eye and I recalled Richard Bach's 1970s classic,* Jonathan Livingston Seagull. *On the surface, it's a story about a seagull's feats of daring and beauty, but it's really a tale of spiritual growth. Soon after reading the book in the '70s, I bought Neil Diamond's album that put the beauty of the story into words and music. Sitting on the beach today, I suddenly yearned to hear that album. Thanks to the modern miracle of iTunes, I listened for a full hour to Neil Diamond's glorious symphonic music. I laughed and cried. I've just returned from the beach, totally filled with inspiration.*

Time for Action!
Tool 36. Your Own Renewal Break

When everything you hear or see appears negative, you'll know you need some time to renew your outlook on life. First, check to see if you're suffering from one or more of the HALTS conditions and take care of them. Then ask yourself if you need a renewal break. If so, follow the directions.

1. Schedule two or three hours when you can be alone and don't have to tend to another's needs. This time is all about you.

2. Let your loved ones and work associates know well in advance that you won't be available to them during the hours of your break.
3. Plan an activity that will feel good without harming others or yourself. You might take a nature walk, have a massage, visit a garden, or go to a movie. Perhaps you'll just lie down and listen to music, or take a hot fragrant bath.
4. Take your renewal break and return to your life refreshed, knowing you have comforted and nurtured yourself.

Your recovery from past wounds will likely look much different than mine. The common thread is this: You'll notice your negative patterns tend to repeat themselves, hindering your happiness and peace of mind.

Delving into the shadows of your past with growth partners, honesty, and power will help you choose a new reality for yourself. Your consistent use of growth tools will bring you a new outlook, intuitive guidance, and freedom from worry. You will indeed be free to express your true self.

Summary

- Your shadow-self contains damaging fears and whispered lies.
- Growth practices and tools harness positive power to dissolve your worries and negative thinking.
- Seek a new perspective instead of letting fear determine your outlook.
- Remember, your old wounds and negative patterns will heal in manageable layers.
- You are responsible for healing the wounds of your past.
- When you feel discouraged about your progress, use growth tools and trust loving power's perfect order.

Chapter 6

Healing Your Relationships

Holding on to old resentments
keeps our creative energy trapped and stifled.
New freedom is the gift we give ourselves
when we choose not to let the sun rise on yesterday's script.
—Anonymous, *Body, Mind, and Spirit*

Do you have a child who drinks too much alcohol, has a drug addiction, or is deeply depressed? Maybe your spouse or partner is unhappy, angry, or ill. Perhaps you've had a hurtful interaction with a friend or coworker. Worries about your loved ones cost you not only your own peace of mind; such fears often prompt controlling behavior that harms these precious relationships.

Using the Four Strategies will transform your connection with the most important people in your life. You'll honestly face and reframe whispered lies such as, "What's wrong with them?" "Why aren't they nicer to me?" or "I can't stand watching them in this dire situation." In most cases, you'll experience face-to-face healing; if not, you'll feel less emotional turmoil and a peaceful acceptance of their choices.

Once again, consider Rumi's quote "Out beyond ideas of wrongdoing and rightdoing is a field. I'll meet you there." When we refuse to let anger, envy, pride, or guilt close our heart toward another, we find a harmonious connection with him in a field of peace.

Some refer to the healing of personal conflict as *forgiveness*. *A Course in Miracles* calls it a miracle. I think of it as dissolving the negativity within to create space for loving feelings and wise actions. Regardless of the words, when you choose to see the best in a person rather than the worst, you heal both yourself and them.

You might be wondering if forgiving someone gives them permission to keep hurting you or others. The answer is no. When you bring positive power into your relationship, you'll know how to respond in the best way for all involved—even if you must set a boundary to stop unacceptable behavior or end the relationship.

My good friend's husband used to frequently launch verbal assaults at her. After years of this abuse, she entered therapy and began to ask him to change his words and tone. Unfortunately, the verbal abuse continued. When she asked him to join her in therapy, he refused. After her threats to seek a divorce, he was more congenial for a while. When he became abrasive again, my friend quietly moved out.

Such assertive action, however, didn't prevent her from seeing the light of her husband's true nature. She felt compassion toward his human failings, held him in her loving thoughts, all while choosing not to tolerate his bad behavior. Ironically, they're better friends now than before.

Repairing troubling relationships is one of life's greatest challenges. In my case, the layers described in chapter 5 healed much of my past. But more remained.

Oh No! Not This!

On his thirtieth birthday, Peter sat without hope on the floor of his old farmhouse. Even though cocaine had emptied his pockets and shredded his self-respect, he couldn't go even a few minutes without snorting it. He held a gun in his shaking hand trying to get the courage to use it.

Instead of pulling the trigger, he called his doctor and entered a drug treatment program. Seven years later, we were married. Shortly after our twentieth anniversary, he decided to have a beer with his golfing buddies.

He told me about it and assured me he had no intention of drinking more than one beer a day.

During the next few months, I thought he had kept his word. Then one night, while setting up the bar for our holiday party, he went to his workshop and returned holding a nearly empty half gallon of vodka. When I asked him about it, he said he'd bought the bottle a month ago, and it was "only sixty-four ounces." I was stunned.

I did the math and my worried mind went into overload, "He's been hiding it. How much is he *really* drinking?" I had spent several years helping friends get clean and sober, and had seen many of them end up in a hospital, jail, or morgue. My terrified mind began replaying these images and projecting future disasters for my husband and me.

Strategy 1. Get Honest—Admit That Your Worries Have Kept You Stuck in Unhappiness

Even though I tried to push what that bottle represented out of my thoughts, I became extremely tense. I once again turned to growth tool 5 to explore the fears underlying my stress.

> **January 4. Journal Entry**
> *Ever since seeing Peter's vodka, I've been picking at my nails and tearing off the polish. I'm terrified Peter's drinking is out of hand and will threaten our marriage. I'm amazed at the power of denial. Wives of alcoholics are often the last to acknowledge the problem. My mother never did. My sister never did. As I watched them, I wondered how they could they be so blind. Now I understand.*

After writing this, I was tempted to crawl under a blanket and hide. But, remembering my recommendation to join with others when facing a challenge, I called a friend who attended Al-Anon meetings. At first, I was relieved to tell someone with a similar experience about my apprehension. But my reaching out only made my situation seem more real—an essential but uncomfortable ingredient of honesty.

Strategy 2. Claim Power—Claim a Source of Positive Power to Overcome Your Worries

I love Twelve-Step meetings because no one gives advice. By merely listening to others' stories and insights, one's perspective changes; suddenly, hope seems possible.

At my first Al-Anon meeting, I heard two helpful things. After sharing concerns about her child's illness, a woman said, "Because I've been through scary things before, and I'm doing something healthy about it, I can feel less shitty about feeling shitty." We all broke out laughing and I felt my burden ease. If she could find hope and humor in her circumstances, so could I in mine.

"We're each surrounded by an imaginary hula hoop," said a veteran Al-Anon member. "We can only control what's inside of it." These words helped me admit that, even though Peter's drinking could threaten the future of our marriage, it was outside my control. When I accepted this fact, I was willing to ask my positive power for peace and guidance, whether the drinking continued or not.

January 6. Journal Entry
I can hear myself trying to figure out how much Peter is drinking.
Is this inside my hula hoop? No. Instead of focusing on him, I need
to take responsibility for what's going on inside my own hula hoop.
Right now, every fiber of my being wants him to stop. Here's my all-
hell-breaks-loose scenario: Peter drinks more and more, becomes
abusive, financially stupid, and/or dies from the disease. OK, I've
shined the flashlight on the fear monster, and my heart is pounding
away in my chest. I really need my loving power to take care of this
because I can't!

I decided to use tapping, tool 21, to stream healing power into my body, mind, and spirit. As I tapped my palms on alternating sides of my thighs, I said aloud, "Even though I'm terrified about Peter's drinking, I love and accept myself completely; and positive power loves and accepts me completely." For the second round, I began, "Even though I'm afraid of losing Peter, I love and accept myself completely . . . " In the third round, I said, "Even though I'm afraid of being alone . . . " As each round progressed, I could feel my terror diminishing.

I then affirmed, "Thank you, loving power, for being with Peter and me. Thank you for my healthy friends' love, strength, and comfort. Please bring this situation into perfect order, even though right now I can't see it." As I said these words, I knew I was doing a bit of faking it, but I said them anyway. Soon I gained the courage to move forward.

Strategy 3. Make Choices—Choose a New Future and Commit to Do the Necessary Work to Achieve It
and
Strategy 4. Use Growth Practices—Consistently Use a Variety of Tools to Dissolve Your Worries

I knew if I tried to address our problems from my current state of fear, I could make things worse—either by trying so hard to control my husband that I damaged our marriage; or by worrying, losing my peace of mind, and putting my own sobriety at risk.

I set a goal to talk with Peter when I could operate from inspiration rather than anxiety. For the next several days, I used almost every growth tool I had to ward off my panic: meditation, prayer, tapping, meeting with my growth partners, self-compassion, gratitude lists, and regular Al-Anon meetings.

Tool 37. Al-Anon: Treatment for Codependence

One definition of *codependence* is doing everything you can to remove the pain or dysfunction from your loved one. People caught in this trap see themselves as victims ("If only he would change, I could be happy,") or martyrs ("I have to take care of him all the time because nobody else will."). They're content only when the other person isn't drinking, overeating, using drugs, overworking, or depressed. But when the person reverts to disturbing behavior, the codependent's serenity evaporates. Such people often suffer from debilitating exhaustion, depression, bitterness, or all of these.

Al-Anon members learn to take care of themselves first, set limits, and allow the dysfunctional person to receive the full consequences of their choices. They do this by following the same Twelve Steps used to treat alcoholism. Codependence is, after all, a form of addiction.

In Step 1, participants honestly admit they can't fix their situation on their own. In Steps 2 and 3, they recognize the need for a power greater than themselves, and ask it to guide them to positive changes. Steps 4–11 include an inventory of character weaknesses and assets; making amends where necessary; and using prayer and meditation. Step 12 promises continuous personal growth through helping others. (The Twelve Steps of Alcoholics Anonymous are in appendix C.)

After attending Al-Anon for a few weeks, I asked Cathy, a faith-filled woman with sparkling blue eyes, to guide me through the steps. She was kind and patient; but most important, at those moments when all I could feel was fear and doubt, she saw a loving power within me working toward the best for all concerned. One of her first suggestions was to pray for Peter.

Tool 38. Praying for Others

Praying for the people you're concerned about is a remarkable means for healing troubled relationships. Simply ask that your loved ones receive everything that will make them happy. It's best to avoid material outcomes; instead, you might say, "Bless (*fill in the blank*) with good physical, mental, spiritual, and emotional health. Please give them financial security, compassion, respect, kindness, joy, contentment, peace, and connection." Then do this every time they enter your mind. This practice erases fear and joins your hearts in Rumi's field of peace.

When I began to pray for my husband, the volume of my whispered lies started to diminish, and I recognized both of us were afraid and imperfect. In time, I could focus on the parts of him I treasured instead of on his drinking and its potential consequences. Soon I was inspired to use one of the most powerful growth tools I've ever encountered.

Tool 39. Master Mind Group

The term *Master Mind* first appeared in Napoleon Hill's 1937 best seller, *Think and Grow Rich*, an early application of the law of attraction to the business world. He defined a Master Mind group as, "The coordination of knowledge and effort of two or more people, who work toward a definite purpose, in the spirit of harmony." Hill wrote that, by joining together, the group accessed the power of a Master Mind.

In the 1980s, Jack Boland, a Detroit-based Unity minister, combined Hill's ideas with AA's Twelve Steps to develop the Master Mind Group guidelines in figure 6.1. You can find such groups at most Unity churches, or you might form one of your own.

---

1. *I Surrender.* I admit that, of myself, I am powerless to solve my problems, powerless to improve my life. I need help.

2. *I Believe.* I come to believe that a power greater than myself, the Master Mind, can change my life.

3. *I Am Ready to Be Changed.* I realize that erroneous self-defeating thinking is the cause of my problems, unhappiness, fears, and failures. I am ready to have my beliefs and attitudes changed so my life can be transformed.

4. *I Decide to Be Changed.* I make a decision to surrender my will and my life to the Master Mind. I ask to be changed at depth.

5. *I Forgive.* I forgive myself for all my mistakes and shortcomings. I also forgive and release all other persons who may have harmed me.

6. *I Ask.* I make known my specific requests, asking my partners' support in knowing that the Master Mind is fulfilling my needs.

7. *I Give Thanks.* I give thanks that the Master Mind is responding to my needs, and I assume the same feelings I would have if my requests were fulfilled.

8. *I Dedicate My Life.* I now have a covenant in which it is agreed that the Master Mind is supplying me with an abundance of all things necessary to live a successful and happy life. I dedicate myself to be of maximum service to God and those around me; to live in a manner that sets the highest example for others to follow; and to remain responsive to God's guidance. I go forth with a spirit of enthusiasm, excitement, and expectancy. I am at peace.

Figure 6.1. The Eight Steps of a Master Mind Group

The positive power marshalled by my Master Mind partners has contributed to many successes in my life: staying sober, building healthy relationships, overcoming illnesses, and writing this book. Our six-person group uses the following format at our weekly ninety-minute sessions.

1. *Check-in.* One at a time, members report on the progress they've made since the last meeting.
2. *Read steps 1–5 aloud.* One person reads the first step aloud. The group members pause, consider the statement, and when ready, each one says, "Yes, I agree."
   - The person to the right of the first person reads step 2 aloud, and all members agree.
   - The next person to the right reads step 3, and all members agree.
   - The same process continues with steps 4 and 5.
3. *Make a request (step 6).* The next person reads step 6 and makes a request: "I ask the Master Mind to . . . " Examples of typical requests include: "I ask the Master Mind to open my heart toward my son-in-law," "I ask for the healing of my fears of the future," "I ask to improve my financial security," and "I ask to be guided toward a safe and affordable place to live."
4. *Affirm the request.* One at a time, each member makes eye contact with the person making the request and says, "I see (*the person's request*) happening for you." Some groups say, "I know the Master Mind has heard you and will provide what you asked for."
5. *Continue making and affirming requests.* One at a time, each member makes a request and the others affirm it. (Some members write down each person's request.)
6. *Read steps 7–8.* The group reads together steps 7 and 8.
7. *Daily follow-up.* Every day, the members visualize and affirm the fulfillment of each person's request.

After Peter began drinking again, I asked my group members to affirm that I would be at peace about his drinking and our future. In later weeks, I asked to know when to talk to him and what to say for the best outcomes for all concerned.

Remembering that each day my partners were supporting my requests gave me great comfort. On the days when I doubted my prayers mattered, I knew my friends' affirmations were getting through. Short electronic messages from them such as, "When going through difficult times, if you feel like your higher power has left you, remember the teacher is always quiet during a test," kept my spirits up.

Time for Action!
Tool 2 (chapter 1). Finding Your Growth Partners

If you spend a lot of time worrying about an important person in your life, you may benefit from joining an established group. Or consider gathering one or two like-minded friends to discuss an inspiring book or follow the Master Mind steps.

1. If appropriate, attend an Al-Anon or Adult Children of Alcoholics meeting. You might find Celebrate Recovery or other faith-based gatherings in houses of worship. The app, Meetup, may list a group that appeals to you. See appendix C for more resources.
2. Review the guidelines at the end of chapter 1 for finding a growth group. Attend at least four meetings before deciding if you want to keep attending.
3. Arrive five minutes early and stay five minutes late. Strike up a conversation with someone who is standing alone or who has said something that piqued your interest. There's little to no benefit for you unless you connect with at least one person in the group.
4. Get phone numbers of people to call when you feel discouraged—or encouraged. Make sure there are no romantic possibilities with the people you select.
5. As you learn or hear about more growth tools, begin to use the ones that appeal to you.

If you detest groups and are facing a significant challenge, I suggest you consult a counselor. Even after surrounding yourself with healthy people, your loved one may continue to harm herself, others, or you. At that point, you will need to set a firm boundary.

Tool 28 (chapter 5). Setting Boundaries

One day in mid-January, my Master Mind request was fulfilled when Jana, my friend from California, called to chat. As I shared with her my worries about Peter's drinking, she said I owed it to him (and to myself) to be honest with him. She helped me clarify what I could and could not live with, and how to approach him.

Later that day, I told him I was concerned his behavior would escalate into full-blown alcoholism. He said he understood. By the end of our talk, we agreed he would have no more than two drinks a day. Our calm and honest conversation was a relief.

As you read in chapter 5, one round of the Four Strategies doesn't always resolve your concerns. Sometimes your situation gets worse before getting better.

It Gets Worse

After our talk, I never saw Peter have more than two drinks, and I felt less concerned about him. In May, he was having difficulty sleeping, and his doctor gave him a new medication. Suddenly, my kind and easygoing husband began to be irritable and curt. When I confronted him about the sharp tone he had used with me, he stormed out the door.

A few nights later, we went to a friend's house where he had two drinks. When we all arrived at the restaurant, he ordered a third cocktail and I panicked. Shortly afterwards, he made a loud disparaging remark about a man at the next table. I hissed, "I can't believe you just said that!" My words fell on drunken ears.

As we left the restaurant, we barely spoke. I drove the car home in spite of his protests.

Strategies 1 and 2: Honesty and Power

I had to face a harsh fact: Peter was drinking more than we had agreed, and his personality was changing.

May 21. Journal Entry

I have never seen Peter seriously inebriated until tonight. It was absolutely shocking! I feel him disappearing, floating off into the distance. With alcohol in him, I don't know who he is. I'm so confused. I can't tell what's real and what's my imagination. Is this "social" drinking or not? Is it the new medication? This has gotten way worse. I'm praying like crazy.

At a restaurant a few days later, he ordered a martini and defiantly asked me, "Does that work for you?" I said, "Not really," and explained my reaction to his previous drunken behavior. He countered with a stony silence. This was a first. During the twenty-three years of our marriage, he had never been sarcastic or shut me out.

Shortly after this event, I returned home from a meeting with a friend. As I turned onto our oak-bowered road, I felt dread deep in my gut: Home didn't feel like a safe place anymore.

Peter was upstairs and didn't acknowledge me when I came in. I called my Al-Anon sponsor, Cathy, and told her I was afraid this unsafe, unhappy feeling would go on forever. She reassured me positive power was working in my marriage, and suggested I continue to pray. So, I rested on my bed, said the Serenity Prayer, and imagined myself surrounded by the protective presence of love.

After a while, Peter came downstairs, found me lying silently on the bed, and asked, "Are you OK?" I said no, and burst into tears. Through my sobs, I told him I felt I had lost my best friend. He took me in his arms and said, "I knew it was bad, but I didn't know it was this bad."

Unfortunately, this moment of connection did not resolve our conflict. He continued to drink an unknown amount and was quite surly. I persisted with the use of my program to calm my fears.

Strategies 3 and 4: Choices and Growth Tools

As I worked the Al-Anon steps, I realized I was attached to an unenforceable rule: "I can only accept being married to a sober man." This belief fueled my codependent concerns and hardened my heart against Peter.

To reframe that lie, Cathy suggested I write down each possible outcome and decide if I could accept it. First, I listed the worst-case scenario: Peter will continue drinking alcoholically and ruin our lives. Two other possibilities came to me: He will stop drinking altogether; or he will become a social drinker, having no more than two drinks a day.

As I considered these options, I realized I could live with any one of them, as long as I had the care of my friends and my loving power. Of course, I wanted to avoid the worst, but I had to admit I wasn't in control.

After sharing my list with Cathy, I set a goal to be peaceful, honest, and courageous with my husband and myself, regardless of the outcome. I wrote affirmations for a happy and harmonious marriage, repeated them often, and created a vision board for that goal. After much prayer, meditation, and work with my growth partners, I felt it was time to have another honest talk with Peter.

Tool 40. Healthy Confrontation

I'm a total coward when it comes to any conversation about a personal conflict. Even though I've learned to do it, my heart pounds and my body shakes. I again consulted my assertive friend, Jana, for help.

The next day at around 11:30 in the morning, I asked Peter if we could talk. He agreed, but our discussion got off to a bad start when I asked him if he'd had anything to drink that day. He roared back, "Your AA friends have convinced you I have a problem when I don't!"

I apologized for starting our conversation that way, and went on to say the words Jana and I had crafted: "I need to tell you how much your increased drinking is upsetting me. We've had such a wonderful life together, and I've loved being with a man who's so kind, patient, and has such a great sense of humor. Now that you've started down this path of drinking, I see our life together fading away. It's tearing me up to stand by and watch it; I don't want us to lose what we have."

I added that, if his drinking got worse and he didn't do anything about it, I could not stay and watch him die. He replied, "Well, if it bothers you so much, I just won't drink in front of you." Later that day, he announced, "Two topics are off-limits: alcohol and health."

The next day, he was withdrawn. When I asked how he was doing, he said our talk had damaged his trust, but the feeling would pass. I responded, "If I gave you the impression I'm about to leave you, that's not true." He replied, "Well, I almost left *you*."

Terrified, I called Cathy and told her I resented him for putting me through so much heartbreak. She suggested that, since I couldn't change Peter, I should look at my own part in my distress.

Tool 41. Housecleaning

Al-Anon's steps 4 through 9, the *housecleaning steps*, helped me find and clear out my most damaging whispered lies. The steps include: sharing one's resentments and fears; accessing positive power to overcome damaging patterns; and making amends to others.

Twelve-Step programs warn that "resentment is the number one offender" to peace of mind and loving relationships. Notice how the word *resentment* implies a repetitive feeling (*re-sentment*) just like a painful song playing incessantly in the mind.

For my own inventory, Cathy asked me to address three questions: What were my resentments and fears? What was it about my past that made this so difficult? What part of my distress was I responsible for?

June 2. My Personal Inventory

I'm angry this is happening to me. I'm afraid of being divorced and alone again. I can't believe I'm married to a man who's drinking alcoholically and who is suddenly so scary to me. The one man I trusted to be kind is just as untrustworthy as my dad. I refuse to be in my mother's position!

I am responsible for believing the following whispered lies:

- *I can't be happy if Peter is drinking.*

- *Men always hurt women! Peter is just like my dad.*

- *Here I go again, failing in my fourth marriage! Something must be wrong with me.*

- *I must defend myself against hurt; nothing can keep me safe.*

I surrender these lies to my loving power so I can find peace and positive direction.

As I shared my inventory with Cathy, I saw I had made my peace of mind contingent on Peter's behavior. I had jumped to the conclusion he would abuse and disappoint me just like my father. Cathy helped me see the solution to my fear and anger was in forgiving myself, Peter, and equally important, my father. I knew I had a long way to go.

Time for Action!
Tool 42. Your Personal Inventory

What relationship frustrations are you harboring? It's important to address them because people who are often angry or hostile are 19 percent more likely to get heart disease; and the angry and hostile with heart problems have a shorter life span, according to research reported by Katherine Kam in *WebMD*.

1. In your journal, create two columns as in the example.
2. On the left side, list three to five people and/or situations you've been angry or frustrated about in the past few weeks.
3. In the right column, write the fears, whispered lies, or worries you've had about the first resentment.
4. Do the same for each of the resentments on your list.
5. If you discover an old wound or another source of anger, add it to the list.

Example

Resentments I'm mad because:	Fears and Whispered Lies
1. (*Fill in the blank*) is being mean to me.	If I say something, he'll leave me. I deserve this kind of treatment.
2. I saw Dad abuse Mom.	I'm insecure and afraid to trust anyone. Men cannot be trusted.
3. My friend has no time for me.	I will be left alone without any friends. I'm not worthy of my friends' time.

6. Now that you've discovered these lies, remember to use the truth phrases in tool 24 to dissolve them.

Sometimes even reprogramming your mind doesn't heal a deep resentment lying in your shadow-self. In such cases, it's best to pursue forgiveness toward yourself and those involved.

You Can Let Go of the Past

As Yoda said in *Star Wars*, "Fear is the path to the dark side. Fear leads to anger. Anger leads to hate. Hate leads to suffering." Quite often, we're unaware of our own anger because we deflect it onto others. We need to, instead, honestly admit our feelings, claim the power to heal a grudge, and open our hearts toward those we've resented.

If forgiveness is the best response to the failures of the important people in our lives, why is it so hard to do? Because it requires letting go of the past. The word *for-give* has two parts: fore (short for before) and give. To those who hurt us in the past *(before)*, we *give* love. When we have achieved forgiveness, we look beyond others' wrongdoing, admit we've made similar errors, and find compassion for our common imperfections.

In William P. Young's best seller, *The Shack*, the main character, Mack, is grief stricken and cannot shake his overwhelming sadness and anger after his daughter is abducted and killed.

One day, he receives a mysterious invitation to go alone to a shack in the woods. When he arrives, a heavyset black woman flings open the door, enfolds him in her arms, and says, "Welcome, Mack! I'm so glad you came!" She asks to be called Papa, the name his lost daughter and wife had used for God. Soon he meets Jesus, a Middle Eastern man wearing a tool belt; and Sarayu, a diaphanous presence of goodness.

Throughout the weekend, these three teach Mack about love and forgiveness. In one scene, Mack goes to a cave to meet Sophia, who is sitting in a large, raised judge's chair. She fixes her eyes on Mack and cautions him not to judge his daughter's death as a tragedy, leaving only pain in its path. Sophia tells him our human perspective is too limited to perceive the perfect order of things; therefore, we need to stop judging others and surrender our thinking to a wiser power.

Later, after Mack asks if he must stop hating the man who killed his daughter, Jesus replies, "Forgiveness is . . . about letting go of another person's throat."

When Mack asks how to do this, Jesus suggests saying, "I forgive you" a hundred times for a few days. He adds that such acts of forgiveness would open his heart and bring God great joy. Mack follows this advice and finds freedom from his overwhelming pain.

The lessons in *The Shack* taught me that love was powerful enough to overcome the whispered lies triggered by Peter's drinking. The next right tool showed up just in time.

Tool 43. Radical Forgiveness

By early July, my husband had returned to his kind self, and hadn't had more than two drinks a day. Still, I was terrified the past would repeat itself.

My childhood had left me with a long-standing resentment toward men who hurt women. For instance, when I saw *Madama Butterfly*, I left extremely disturbed by the callous treatment of the soldier toward his beautiful Asian lover. Or, when I heard a story about spousal abuse, I became unusually enraged and could not let it go. I recognized my distrust of men had spilled over into my marriage.

One day, my friend, Richard, ran across a parking lot to tell me I absolutely had to read Colin Tipping's *Radical Forgiveness*. Tipping presents the radical idea that our painful experiences are designed *to bring to the surface and dissolve the false beliefs blocking the expression of our best self.* His worksheets reprogram one's thoughts about—and reactions to—past painful relationships.

Soon after reading the book, I completed the Radical Forgiveness Worksheet in appendix A. Here's a short summary.

1. *Tell the story.* I was upset about Peter's escalating alcohol use and worried it would ruin our lives.

2. *Feel the feelings.* I stopped judging my feelings and admitted they were simply a reflection of my perception of the situation. My discomfort was evidence of my own need to change.

3. *Collapse the story.* I identified the beliefs that had kept me stuck: "People always hurt me," "You can't trust men," and "Life's not fair and I must suffer." I gave myself permission to release these lies.

4. *Do a radical forgiveness reframe.* I saw my soul had created this situation to help me heal the belief I was a helpless victim of men's mistreatment. I realized that I was loved and cared for, regardless of my father's abuse and Peter's current actions. My true nature empowered me to feel love for all of us.

5. *Integration.* I gave thanks to my husband for playing a part in alerting me to my resentment toward my father. I began repeating, "I forgive you, Dad." Turning my attention to Peter, I saw that his negative behavior had ceased. I also thanked myself for going through this tough time without using drugs or alcohol.

After completing the worksheet, I copied and laminated some of its affirmations and put them in my purse. Every time I started to worry, I read those words and affirmed their truth. After sharing my insights with my sponsor, I wrote in my journal.

July 15. Journal Entry

When I left home today to meet some friends for lunch, I listened to Colin Tipping's CD, Radical Self-Forgiveness which melted away all my resistance, sadness, and regret. I had a palpable sensation of loving power flowing into me, releasing my father, Peter, and me from resentment and conflict. I forgave us all for having such a difficult time together.

Tool 44. Making Amends

After using these tools, I finally found peace, and was ready to make amends for my part in our challenges.

Later that week, as we were preparing dinner, I remarked, "I had an important insight this week. I realized I've held a lot of anger toward men who hurt women, especially toward my dad. During our many years together, I had never put you in that category. But, during the past months, I did just that and I apologize. I can see how you would be insulted that I thought you were that way." Afterward, we had a long discussion to begin rebuilding the trust we had lost.

My husband's drinking served as a catalyst to heal a deep resentment toward my father, lying in my shadow-self. My personal inventory, radical forgiveness, and making amends helped me focus on the light of our true natures, the perfection of our human struggles, and the healing love in and around us.

It's been over five years since those troubling months. In contrast to what happens with most addicts, Peter drinks alcohol only occasionally and in moderation; and he's returned to being kind and fun. Maybe getting older has played a part, or stopping the sleeping medication. In the final analysis, however, I give credit to my loving power for saving our marriage.

I can't say I never experience frustration or annoyance toward my husband, friends, colleagues, or family. But, when I do, I'm able to pause and consider the damage done by unresolved resentments. I then try to identify them, and work toward acceptance and compassion.

Time for Action!
Tool 45. Forgiveness Checkup

Here you'll replace unforgiving thoughts and habits with loving ones.

1. Read the items in both columns and place a check next to the ways you typically respond to troubling relationships and situations.
2. Give yourself kudos and appreciation for the ones you checked on the right side.
3. If you checked anything on the left side, choose from the right side the new response you wish to demonstrate.

4. Create an affirmation to reinforce your choice, and invite your loving power to remove all barriers to your goal. Consistently use growth tools to bring healing into your life and relationships. As new insights or difficulties arise, address them with honesty, power, choices, and more growth practices. Remember, you are seeking progress, not perfection.

Non-Forgiveness (Worry and Fear)	Forgiveness (Peace and Joy)
Resentment or anger	Freedom to give and receive love
Judging others and myself	Seeing loving power in others and myself
Hating and attacking through words or thoughts	Remaining openhearted and compassionate toward others
Thinking I would be better than that (Pride)	Realizing that we all make mistakes (Humility)
Resisting life through frustration or irritability	Accepting life by being in the present moment
Wishing things were different and attaching to those outcomes	Trusting perfect order through nonattachment
Defensiveness and insecurity	Peace, trust, and courage

No discussion of forgiveness is complete without mentioning the ancient Hawaiian practice *ho'oponopono*. Although it began as a spiritual healing ritual for families in conflict, it's been distilled into a simple mantra: "I love you. I'm sorry. Please forgive me. Thank you."

Joe Vitale and Ihaleakala Hew Len's book, *Zero Limits: The Secret Hawaiian System for Wealth, Health, Peace & More*, presents this powerful practice to replace resentment with joy and connection—the goal of all important relationships.

Summary

- Your relationship worries pose an invitation to heal the whispered lies that block your vitality, love, and joy.
- Resentment hardens your heart toward others and keeps good from entering your life.
- Forgiveness occurs when you let go of anger and accept the person you resented with an open heart.
- Forgiveness doesn't prevent you from setting a boundary or ending a relationship.
- Joining with others helps you heal old wounds and forgive your past.

Chapter 7

Reaping the Rewards:
Peace, Clarity, and Connection

You and I were put on this earth
to serve something greater than our narrow interests.
—Nick Vujicic, *Unstoppable: The Incredible Power*
of Faith in Action

In David Michie's charming book, *The Dalai Lama's Cat*, a self-development celebrity confesses to the Dalai Lama that he can no longer teach others that wealth and success bring happiness. The Dalai Lama replies that there are "Two main true causes of happiness: first, the wish to give happiness to others . . . and second, the wish to help free others from dissatisfaction or suffering. . . . The more we can focus our thoughts on the well-being of others, the happier we become." The man left realizing, "Self-Development takes us only so far. Then there needs to be Other Development."

If helping others is so valuable, why is it so difficult to do? Humans have been seeking moral correction for our inherent self-centeredness for thousands of years through religion, philosophy, and art. Clearly, it's no easy task.

Figure 7.1 illustrates how the Four Strategies transform a fearful, self-serving life into a generous and satisfying one. Saturated with the message of a never-enough world, our initial focus is competing with, trying to control, or blaming others.

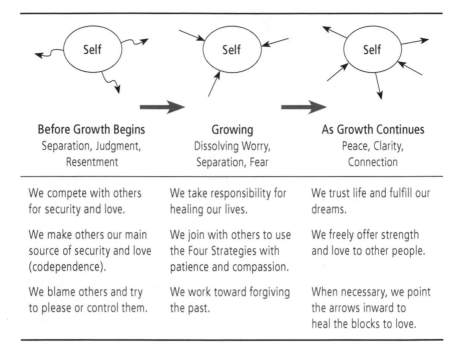

Figure **7.1.** Transforming from a Fearful Person to a Loving Person

As we invest in our growth, we begin taking responsibility for our own choices, beliefs, and actions. The right people and resources appear as the flow of positive power becomes a part of us.

We eventually leave our old patterns behind to gain peace, attain our dreams, and freely offer strength and love to others. We look inward from time to time to check for and heal any new obstructions to love.

Every time I've faced a daunting challenge or growth period, I've gone through these stages. At first, fear pushes me back into selfishness and resentment, but as I use the strategies and tools, I work through my difficulties and reap the benefits.

You can gain these same rewards:

- *Peace of mind,* wisdom, hope, and gratitude for life, no matter your situation;

- *Clarity* so you can fulfill your dreams without limitations; and
- *Connection* through service to others and thriving relationships.

Peace of Mind: Trust Life

When your troubles plunge you into agitation, they whisper you can't be at peace until they're fixed. Unfortunately, this approach is upside down. Only after seeking peace of mind will the best solutions appear. It sounds easy but requires great patience. As Amma, the hugging saint says, "Love is like the blossoming of a flower. You cannot force it to open."

Pretend you've planted a seed. Each day you water it and check its progress. A green stem eventually sprouts from the earth, and then a pale pink bud emerges. Suddenly, you have an insane urge to pry it open and see it in full bloom; instead you choose to patiently continue caring for it. Your reward is a fragrant, beautiful flower; and recognition that—from flowers to human experiences—each miracle appears in its own time and its own way.

Peace of mind is like waiting for the blossom to appear. In the meantime, you remind yourself that, no matter how scary a situation appears, your positive power's strength and wisdom will resolve it. You practice nonattachment, use growth tools, and wait.

There's a perfect order to the events in our lives that often isn't clear until time reveals its elegant solutions. What initially seemed to be my worst disasters yielded some of my greatest blessings; but these gifts appeared in their own time.

- Alcoholism brought me a spiritual path, healthy friends, a happy marriage, and creative productivity.
- Many years of shoulder and back pain taught me to accept what I couldn't change, to trust positive power, and accept care and comfort from others.
- My husband's resumption of drinking resulted in my forgiving my father and a new appreciation for my marriage.

While I don't relish such challenges, I've learned that each upsetting event or person will ultimately increase my growth and ability to love.

Time for Action!
Tool 46. Are All Hard Times Totally Bad?

It's easier to cope with life when you trust something better is coming, even though you can't yet perceive it. When you see ups and downs as opportunities to grow, you can relax and enjoy life.

1. Think of a few major life challenges in your past.
2. List two or three of them in your journal, leaving space to write under each one.
3. Beneath each life challenge, describe the subsequent benefits it brought you and your loved ones.
4. Now consider two problems worrying you. Write them down, along with their possible positive outcomes.

When a person—or life—pushes your buttons, it's a chance to face and heal old beliefs that no longer serve you. Especially when you repeatedly receive—and accept—the same poor treatment, it's a wake-up call. As you choose to do the work to overcome the pattern, you'll experience an exhilarating freedom.

Clarity: Fulfill Your Dreams

What are your most cherished dreams? When the flow of power opens your life channel, you'll intuitively know which ones to pursue because *your true self knows what's right for you.*

Unfortunately, we don't receive written instructions for our future. But we *do* get glimmers and guideposts if we clear our minds of fear and pay attention. Throughout these pages, you've read about my experience with mysterious coincidences.

- I was able to explore and attain forgiveness after a friend I hadn't seen in months ran across a parking lot to give me a book on that very topic.

- I began to meditate regularly after several chance encounters with others who had benefitted from meditating.
- Lunch with a friend turned into a connection with her aunt whose energy psychology techniques helped me overcome my writer's block.

As you become more receptive to your true self, you'll notice little signals from the universe that guide you, whether it's a big decision or a little one.

When you're totally confused about which way to go, take a moment to breathe, be honest with yourself, claim your power, and choose to take just one step forward. The first step you take is like holding a flashlight that illuminates only a few feet in front of you. You can't see where you're headed, but you can see the next step, and know that taking one step is enough for now.

Sometimes the only way to tell if you're on the right track is to make the decision to go forward; then, stop and listen to your inner compass—the quiet voice inside that tells the truth. Is it saying you're on track? Remember, you have the right to say no and the right to change your mind. So, even if you discover you've taken the wrong path, you *can change your direction.*

Occasionally it's hard to distinguish an old whispered lie from a reasonable doubt. But, if you stay present with yourself, you can sense fear's devious tone, reject it, and open the way for intuition to enter your mind.

Time for Action!
Tool 47. Your Meaningful Coincidences

Take time to listen to the voice of your inner guide. For instance, with your coat on and preparing to leave your house, you might get a nudge in your gut that you're missing your keys. Instead of dismissing the idea, you stop, realize it's true, get them, and give thanks for the gift of that little signal.

1. At the beginning of each day, state an intention to notice meaningful coincidences and intuitive nudges.

2. At the end of the day, describe these events in your journal along with their outcomes. Give thanks for the presence of miracles in your life.
3. Note how, over time, your coincidences and intuitive guidance increase.

As you tune in to the wisdom of your true self, you'll find an ally that gives you valuable direction in any circumstance. And you'll be guided to fulfill your most magnificent dreams.

Connection: Give and Receive Love

No matter how we express love to another, we always benefit. In the words of a Chinese proverb, "The fragrance always stays in the hand that gives the rose." When we extend kindness, we gain much more than we give; it comes back to us tenfold.

As many wisdom traditions teach, we're all connected and the decisions made by one of us affect not only ourselves, but also *everyone around us*. How can this be? In any social group—from the spiritually inclined to street gangs—the behavior of the key members drives the behavior of others in the group. We either spread love or fear into the people around us. In turn, they affect their own friends and families, and the circle of influence expands.

We learn to give and receive love through relationships because we are both student and teacher to one another. Imagine people holding hands while climbing a hill. The first person leads the person behind him, this person helps the one behind him, and so on. We continue to grow so we can serve others.

You can transmit the power of love in many ways. It may be as simple as a smile or compliment given to the person at a checkout counter. In Christian and other traditions, it's through prayer or healing touch. Teachers such as the Dalai Lama or Amma offer rapt attention or a hug. My friend in the Oneness Movement gives a blessing hug or *deeksha*.

When I've received these concentrated bursts of love from any of these sources, it's always brought me closer to my purpose: to expand peace and kindness.

Receiving

Some say you can only love others if you begin by loving yourself. Others believe you must give love *first* to receive it. It's probably a bit of both. In healthy relationships, sometimes you're the strong one who offers comfort and assistance. At other times, you're on the receiving end.

In *The Answer Is Simple: Love Yourself, Live Your Spirit!*, the spiritual teacher, Sonia Choquette, poses a question that stopped me in my tracks: How easy is it for you to receive from others?

I had to confess that I found it difficult to ask for or accept help. The shame lurking in my unconscious told me I wasn't worth someone's time or attention. As a codependent, it was easier to be a caregiver rather than to accept care from another.

If we don't feel worthy of help from others, we keep track of favors and worry about paying them back. Instead, we could consider all good deeds as "paying it forward." No matter who offers care or love, these acts get "deposited" into a great fund of goodness. When we need help, the fund delivers a benefit, often from an unexpected source.

Take a moment to consider your own willingness to receive from others. It took me a while, but I'm happy to report I'm finally comfortable with it.

Time for Action!
Tool 48. How Good Are You at Receiving?

Write in your journal the answers to the following questions.

1. How easy is it for you to ask others for help?
2. Do you believe you always need to appear strong and competent?
3. Are you most comfortable in the role of helping others?
4. Can you graciously accept healthy loving care regardless of where it comes from?

5. What whispered lies stand in the way of you being a better receiver?

Perhaps you believe no one can be trusted and you must be in control. Or you might think you don't deserve others' support. If necessary replace these—or other mistaken beliefs—with the truths you've garnered from using the tools in this book.

Caring Communication

Giving your complete attention to another person's words offers him a treasure—a sincere gesture of care. Unfortunately, most of us respond to our loved ones either by telling stories about our own past or offering solutions. Both types of responses prevent *seeking to understand first*, perhaps the most important of Stephen Covey's *The 7 Habits of Highly Effective People*.

When in a conversation with someone, open your heart, empty your mind, and *listen*. If you notice yourself thinking about your own past, refocus your attention on what he is saying. If you're tempted to suggest solutions, remind yourself that actively listening is your goal. To show your intent to understand, briefly summarize what you think you heard. After that person's reply, summarize again. Listening in this way not only shows that you care—it also invites the person to clarify his own thoughts and feelings, often leading to helpful insights.

For example, if a friend tells you she's worried about losing her job because her boss constantly criticizes her, tune in, breathe, and resist the urge to tell your own tale about a bad boss. Then paraphrase her words: "It sounds like you get a lot of negative responses from him." Your friend replies, "Well, it's not really criticism. It's just that he has such high expectations." Then you summarize (without giving advice), "Hmmm, high expectations. That's gotta be hard!" This reply elicits her feelings and encourages more detail, allowing both of you to explore the problem and find positive ways to address it.

Another aspect of caring communication involves choosing your words. Certain simple words can empower both yourself and the person you're communicating with—a great gift to anyone. Other words, however, may have a limiting effect on growth.

Change *But* to *And*

Using the word *and* instead of *but* softens statements. While it's easy to follow *but* with criticism or harsh words, it's almost impossible to say anything negative after the word *and*.

Examples

I like her, *but* she talks a lot. ➡ I like her, *and* I've noticed she talks a lot.

I'm not sure about that, *but* I think . . . ➡ I'm not sure about that, *and* I think . . .

You did that well, *but* you should have . . . ➡ You did that well, *and* consider trying this . . .

Use *Yet* or *Up until Now*

I often hear language that assumes a whispered lie is permanent, that no possibility for change exists. Instead of using words that limit one's future, try saying *yet* or *up until now* to create a sense of possibility.

Examples

I'm just not good at that. ➡ I'm not good at that *yet*.

You've always been afraid of risk. ➡ *Up until now*, you've been afraid of risk.

Use Together: *Both, And*

Black-and-white thinking can be unrealistic because people and situations are not usually just one way or another; they're often a bit of both. Growth involves embracing the gray hues of life's uncertainty. Using *both* along with *and* can help us accept the complexity of life.

Examples

I'm so selfish. ➡ I'm *both* selfish *and* generous.

You're either totally afraid or full of courage. ➡ You're *both* afraid *and* courageous.

Change Self-Focus to Other-Focus

Sometimes you'll feel trapped by the whispered lies, "Poor me!" and "No one understands me." You may want to isolate and nurse your wounds, which will *reward* the lies. Ironically, the antidote to a "pity party" is giving loving attention to another—no strings attached. Placing your focus on someone else moves the spotlight away from your own troubles, dissolves emotional isolation, and refreshes your perspective.

During your next conversation with an acquaintance or loved one, try seeking to understand their words. As you practice the art of active listening, you'll find it empowers both of you!

Time for Action!
Tool 49. Truly Listening

1. Select a friend, growth partner, or coworker who is easy to talk to.
2. Plan at least a fifteen-minute conversation without interruption.
3. You may want to begin by explaining that you're working on your listening skills, and reassure the person you have only good intentions—to understand what they say.
4. Ask the person to begin talking about something happening in their life.
5. Listen intently while resisting your urge to break in with your own experiences or solutions.
6. When the person stops, pause to see if they've finished talking and take a moment to prepare your response. Select the most important parts of what was said and summarize one of them in your own words—for example, "So, you said (*fill in blank*). Tell me more about that." or "You mentioned the word (*fill in blank*). What does that mean to you?" Use other positive communication tools you've learned when appropriate.

7. If it seems acceptable to the other person, ask how it felt to be listened to this way.

8. In your everyday interactions, make a conscious effort to listen carefully to others and paraphrase what you heard. Withhold your own thoughts and reactions until you fully comprehend the other person's position or experience.

Even though the habit of seeking to understand may feel artificial, you will soon find it more natural, especially when you sincerely intend to give pure, loving attention to another. As you listen fully, you'll be astonished at how much you learn and by the good will you create.

Keep Growing

One way to ensure consistent growth is to avoid backsliding into worrying and negativity. If you examine, with rigorous honesty, the motives behind your thoughts and actions, you'll uncover the whispered lies that hinder the flow of love into and out of your life.

Although it can be painful to recognize your flaws, please know *they are not permanent and not a complete picture of the person you are.* They're merely habits, conditioned by your past experiences.

I've modified this daily inventory from Twelve-Step programs to help you periodically take stock of your progress.

Time for Action!
Tool 50. Inventory of Assets and Liabilities

Use the table to assess your personal assets and liabilities. You'll want to strengthen your best qualities and use the Four Strategies to change your negative feelings, beliefs, and behaviors. This work produces serenity, joy, and caring relations.

1. Write in your journal the assets you recognize in yourself and give thanks for them.

2. Write in your journal the liabilities you recognize in yourself.

Assets	Liabilities
Self-acceptance	Shame
Self-compassion	Self-condemnation
Humility and Acceptance	Pride, Judgment, and Resistance
Forgiveness	Resentment and Anger
Caring about Others	Selfish and Self-seeking
Gratitude	Envy and Jealousy
Positive Action	Lazy (Sloth) and Avoidance
Honesty	Dishonesty with Self and Others
Courage	Fear of Life
Hope	Despair
Faith	Doubt
Joy	Sadness
Giving Comfort/Love to Others	Seeking only My Own Comfort/Love
Seeking to Understand Others	Seeking only Understanding from Others
Trusting You Have "Enough"	Fear of "Not Enough"

3. List the three liabilities you most want to overcome. For each one, describe in detail
   a) how it interferes with your relationships and life, and
   b) how you and your loved ones' lives would be better without it.
4. Next to each liability you want to change, write its corresponding asset from the right column.
5. Discuss what you wrote with a growth partner, minister, therapist, or someone else you trust. After this courageous conversation, you might add or change some qualities on your list.
6. As described in chapter 4 (tool 16), write affirmations for the assets you'd like to increase or acquire. Visualize yourself as already having them, detach from the details, and use tools such as meditation to access positive power.

7. Every day or week, assess your progress and check in with your growth partners. Set new goals for even more freedom, peace, and happiness.

You'll emerge from your old patterns gradually, and at a perfect pace. Eventually, you'll find yourself acting in new positive ways; even more amazing, the people around you will begin to change, too. It's that "circle of influence" I mentioned earlier. Never underestimate the power of an individual's positive growth.

Parting Words

I hope the Four Strategies and other practices help you find comfort and strength as you grow away from your worries. When you feel upset, connect with your source of positive power, choose to heal the thoughts blocking your peace of mind, and then select and use one or two helpful growth tools to bring joy into your being.

Freeing yourself from destructive thoughts allows the light of your true nature to shine through—to enrich your own life and the lives of those around you.

I hope the following poem, *The Guest House* by Rumi, encourages you in your journey to become peaceful, enjoy clarity, and create loving connections.

This being human is a guest house.
Every morning a new arrival.

A joy, a depression, a meanness,
some momentary awareness comes
As an unexpected visitor.

Welcome and entertain them all!
Even if they're a crowd of sorrows,
who violently sweep your house
empty of its furniture,

still treat each guest honorably.
He may be clearing you out
for some new delight.

The dark thought, the shame, the malice,
meet them at the door laughing,
and invite them in.

Be grateful for whoever comes,
because each has been sent
as a guide from beyond.

A teaching story translated by Coleman Barks © by owner.

Appendix A
The Radical Forgiveness Worksheet

The Radical Forgiveness Worksheet:
An Instrument for the True Transformation
of a Grievance

1. The situation around which I have an upset is (or was). (*Story described in chapter 6.*)

2A. Confronting: I'm upset with you, <u>Peter</u>, because <u>you've been irritable and your drinking has been escalating.</u>

2B. Because of this, I feel <u>disappointed, terrified, angry, and worried.</u>

Acknowledging My Own Humanness

3. I lovingly recognize and accept my feelings, and judge them no more. I'm entitled to my feelings. <u>Yes, I'm open to this idea.</u>

4. I own my feelings. No one can make me feel anything. My feelings are a reflection of how I see the situation. <u>Yes, I'm open to this idea.</u>

5. My discomfort was my signal that I was withholding love from myself and <u>Peter</u> by judging, holding expectations, wanting <u>Peter</u> to change, and seeing <u>Peter</u> as less than perfect.

I've been worried and angry in spite of all my growth tools. Yes,
I need help.

Now Collapsing the Story

6. I now realize that in order to feel the experience more deeply,
    my soul has encouraged me to create a *bigger* story out of the
    event or situation than it actually seemed to warrant, consider-
    ing just the facts.
    He's abandoned me. Alcohol is more important to him than I am.
    Level of Emotion Now: *High*
    He'll never stop. It'll only get worse. Level of Emotion Now: *High*
    This purpose having been served, I can now release the
    energy surrounding my story by separating the facts from
    the interpretations I have made up about it.

7. *Core negative beliefs I either made up from my story or which*
    drove the story (check those that apply):
    ✓ *People always hurt me.*
    ✓ *It is not safe to speak out.*
    ✓ *Life's not fair. I must suffer.*

Now Opening to a Reframe

8. I now realize that my soul encouraged me to form these beliefs
    in order to magnify my sense of separation so I could feel it more
    deeply for my spiritual growth. As I now begin to remember the
    truth of who I am, I give myself permission to let them go, and I
    now send love and gratitude to myself and *Peter* for creating the
    growth experience. *I'm open to this idea.*

Noticing a Pattern
and Seeing the Perfection in It

9. *I recognize that my* Spiritual Intelligence has created stories in the
    past that are similar in circumstance and feeling to this one in
    order to magnify the emotional experience of separation that my
    soul wanted. I'm seeing this as evidence that, even though I don't

know why or how, my soul has created this particular situation, too, in order that I learn and grow. *I'm open to this idea.*
List similar stories and feeling experiences, and note common elements in them.
Alcoholism in my home. Emotionally unavailable mother, and father who harmed me.
Common element: I'm a victim. I have no control.

10. I now realize that I get upset only when someone resonates in those parts of me I have disowned, denied, repressed, and then projected onto them. I see now the truth in the adage, "If you spot it, you've got it!" *I'm open to this idea.*

11. *Peter* is reflecting what I need to love and accept in myself. Thank you, *Peter*, for this gift. I'm now willing to take back the projection and own it as part of my shadow. I love and accept this part of me. *I'm open to this idea.*

12. Even though I may not understand it all, I now realize that you and I have both been receiving exactly what we each had sub-consciously chosen and we're doing a dance with and for each other to bring us to a state of awakened consciousness. *I'm open to this idea.*

13. I now realize that nothing you, *Peter*, have done is either right or wrong. I'm *willing* to see the perfection in the situation just the way it is. *I'm open/skeptical to this idea.*

14. I'm willing to see that, for whatever reason, my mission or "soul contract" included having experiences like this and that you and I may have agreed to do this dance with and for each other in this lifetime. If it is for the highest good for both of us, I now release you and me from that contract. *I'm open to this idea.*

15. I release from my consciousness all feelings of: *Rage, confusion, terror, judgment, arrogance.*

The Reframe Statement

16. The story in item 1 was your Victim Story, based on the old par-adigm of reality (victim consciousness). Now attempt a different

perception of the same event (a reframe), from your new empowered position, based on the insights you have experienced as you
have proceeded through this worksheet. It may simply be a general statement indicating that you just know everything is perfect, or a statement that includes things specific to your situation,
if, that is, you can actually see what the perfection is. Often you
cannot. Be careful not to do a reframe that is based in "world of
humanity" terms. Note any positive shift in feeling love. *I'm loved
and cared for regardless of Peter's actions. I have love and abundance. I trust that everything is in perfect order.*

17. I completely forgive myself, *Gigi*, and accept myself as a loving,
    generous, and creative being. I release all need to hold onto
    emotions and ideas of lack and limitation connected to the past.
    I withdraw my energy from the past and release all barriers I
    had against the love and abundance that I know I have in this
    moment. I create my life and am empowered to be myself again,
    to unconditionally love and support myself, just the way I am in
    all my power and magnificence. *I agree.*

18. I now *surrender* to loving power and trust in the knowledge that
    this situation will continue to unfold perfectly and in accor-
    dance with Divine guidance and spiritual law. I acknowledge my
    Oneness and feel myself totally reconnected with my Source.
    I'm restored to my true nature, which is *love*, and I now restore
    love to *Peter*. I close my eyes in order to feel the *love* that flows in
    my life and to feel the joy that comes when the love is felt and
    expressed. *I agree.*

19. A Note of Appreciation and Gratitude to *Peter*: Having done this
    worksheet, I *Gigi*, know that I'm fully receiving and transmitting
    Love. I completely forgive you, *Peter*, for I now realize that you did
    nothing wrong and everything is in Divine order. I bless you for
    being willing to play a part in my awakening—thank you—and
    honor myself for being willing to play a part in your awakening.
    I acknowledge and accept you just the way you are. I agree.

20. A Note to Myself: *Gigi, I love, honor, and thank you for sticking with me through this tough time; and for not using drugs, alcohol, or anger to ruin our life.* I recognize that I'm a spiritual being having a spiritual experience in a human body, and I love and support myself in every aspect of my humanness. *I agree.*

Note: Colin Tipping has approved my use of this example.

Appendix B
Four Strategies and 50 Tools to Worry Less Now

Four Strategies to Overcome Worry

Get Honest	Admit that your worries have kept you stuck in unhappiness.
Claim Power	Claim a source of positive power to overcome your worries through your mind, spirit, or body energy.
Make Choices	Choose a new future and commit to do the necessary work to achieve it.
Use Growth Practices	Consistently use a variety of tools to dissolve your worries. As you gain a peaceful perspective, you will act with wisdom, heal past wounds, repair relationships, and find true happiness.

Growth Practices and Tools

Chapter 1. Four Powerful Strategies to Overcome Worry

1. Mindfulness Meditation
2. Finding Your Growth Partners
3. Your Worries and Their Consequences

Chapter 2. Getting Honest about Your Worries

4. Two Sides of the Coin
5. Journal Writing or Drawing
6. Is It True?
7. Self-Compassion
8. The Balcony View

Chapter 3. Claiming Positive Power

9. Your Positive Power
10. Focusing on Loved Ones
11. Appreciating Beauty
12. Acts of Kindness
13. Inspirational Reading
14. The Serenity Prayer
15. Gratitude List

Chapter 4. Choosing a New Future

16. Your Affirmation
17. Detaching from Outcomes
18. Daily Quiet Time
19. Loving-Kindness Practice
20. Meditation
21. Tapping Therapy
22. The Activity of God Affirmation

Chapter 5. Using Growth Practices to Recover Your True Self

23. The Golden Key
24. Substituting Truth Phrases for Whispered Lies
25. Self-Nurturing
26. Group Therapy
27. Writing an Unsent Letter
28. Setting Boundaries
29. Energy Healing

Appendix C
Suggested Resources

Personal Development

Online Resources

- Tut.com. "Thoughts Become Things: Choose the Good Ones." Mike Dooley, founder. Daily inspirational emails and other enlightening information
- *"Healing with the Masters,"* Jennifer McLean. Webcast and YouTube interviews with personal development experts. healingwiththemasters.com
- Oprah Winfrey and Deepak Chopra's 21-Day Meditation Experience. Free online at chopracentermeditation.com.
- Jack Boland. Compelling teacher of spiritual principles. Deceased Unity minister. Many talks available on YouTube.

Courses

- Mindfulness Based Stress Reduction (MBSR). Jon Kabat-Zinn PhD, developer (University of Massachusetts Medical School). Course offered all over the world. Benefits both physical and mental well-being. Best to take the course in person. umassmed .edu/cfm/mindfulness-based-programs.
- Chopra Center. Resources for meditation and personal growth. chopra.com.

Authors and Books

- Karen Casey. Prolific writer about spiritual growth, recovery, codependence, healing, and A Course in Miracles. womens -spirituality.com
- Anne Lamott. Hilarious, inspiring, disarmingly honest author of books about life and writing. facebook.com/AnneLamott
- The Art of Possibility: Transforming Professional and Personal Life. Rosamund Stone Zander and Benjamin Zander. Penguin, 2002. Observations on art, business, freedom, and assumptions about the everyday world.
- Conversations with God. Book 1. An Uncommon Dialog. Neale Donald Walsch. G.P. Putnam's Sons, 1996. New perspectives on spirituality and love.
- Essential Spirituality. Roger Walsh. Wiley, 2000. Practices to awaken the heart and mind.
- The Four Agreements: A Practical Guide to Personal Freedom, Don Miguel Ruiz. Amber-Allen Publishing, 1997. Basics for good living.
- Pocketful of Miracles. Joan Borysenko. Grand Central Publishing, 1994. Daily meditations from various spiritual and religious traditions.
- Quiet: The Power of Introverts in a World That Can't Stop Talking, Susan Cain. Broadway Books, 2013. Helpful for highly sensitive people.
- Spirit Junkie: A Radical Road to Self-Love and Miracles. Gabrielle Bernstein. Random House, 2011. Autobiographical journey from addiction to spiritual freedom.
- A Twelve-Power Meditation Exercise. Charles Roth. Unity, 2005. Developed by Unity cofounder, Charles Fillmore.

Feminine Aspect of Positive Power

- The Feminine Dimension of the Divine, Joan Chamberlain Engelsman. Chiron Publications, 1994.

- *The Feminine Face of God: The Unfolding of the Sacred in Women.* Sherry Ruth Anderson and Patricia Hopkins. Bantam, 1992.
- *Embracing the Feminine Nature of the Divine.* Toni G. Boehm. Inner Visioning Press, 2001.

Alcoholism, Addiction, Family Codependence

Books

- *It Takes a Family: A Cooperative Approach to Lasting Sobriety.* Debra Jay. Hazelden Publishing, 2014. For family and loved ones of alcoholics and addicts.
- *Stage II Recovery: Life Beyond Addiction.* Earnie Larsen. HarperOne, 2013. Overcoming character flaws.

Groups for Addicts and Alcoholics

- Celebrate Recovery. Christ-centered recovery. celebraterecovery.com
- Refuge Recovery. Buddhist-based recovery. refugerecovery.org
- SMART Recovery. Self-empowering alternative to AA. smartrecovery.org
- Twelve-Step Recovery Groups. Alcoholics Anonymous (aa.org), Narcotics Anonymous (na.org), Gamblers Anonymous (gamblersanonymous.org), Overeaters Anonymous (oa.org), Debtors Anonymous (debtorsanonymous.org).

Groups for Loved Ones of Addicts and Alcoholics

- Al-Anon Family Groups. Twelve-Step meetings. al-anon.org
- Adult Children of Alcoholics. Meetings for people who grew up in alcoholic and other types of dysfunctional families. adultchildren.org

The Twelve Steps of Alcoholics Anonymous
(Alcoholics Anonymous World Services, Inc.)

1. We admitted we were powerless over alcohol—that our lives had become unmanageable.
2. Came to believe that a Power greater than ourselves could restore us to sanity.
3. Made a decision to turn our will and our lives over to the care of God *as we understood Him.*
4. Made a searching and fearless moral inventory of ourselves.
5. Admitted to God, to ourselves, and to another human being the exact nature of our wrongs.
6. Were entirely ready to have God remove all these defects of character.
7. Humbly asked Him to remove our shortcomings.
8. Made a list of all persons we had harmed, and became willing to make amends to them all.
9. Made direct amends to such people wherever possible, except when to do so would injure them or others.
10. Continued to take personal inventory and when we were wrong promptly admitted it.
11. Sought through prayer and meditation to improve our conscious contact with God *as we understood Him,* praying only for knowledge of His will for us and the power to carry that out.
12. Having had a spiritual awakening as the result of these steps, we tried to carry this message to alcoholics, and to practice these principles in all our affairs.

Bibliography

Anonymous. *Body, Mind, and Spirit: Daily Meditations*. Center City, MN: Hazelden, 1990.

Aron, Elaine. *The Highly Sensitive Person: How to Thrive When the World Overwhelms You*. New York: Broadway Books, 1997.

Bach, Richard. *Jonathon Livingston Seagull*. Reissue ed. New York: Scribner, 2014.

Benor, Daniel. *Seven Minutes to Natural Pain Release*. Fulton, CA: Elite Books, 2008.

Boland, Jack. *Master Mind Goal Achievers Journal*. Warren, MI: Master Mind Publishing Company, 1992. https://www.renaissanceunity.org/discover/master-mind-principle.

Borysenko, Joan. *Pocketful of Miracles: Prayer, Meditations, and Affirmations to Nurture Your Spirit Every Day of the Year*. New York: Grand Central Publishing, 1994.

Brown, Brené. *Daring Greatly: How the Courage to Be Vulnerable Transforms the Way We Live, Love, Parent, and Lead*. New York: Avery, 2015.

———. *The Gifts of Imperfection: Let Go of Who You Think You're Supposed to Be and Embrace Who You Are*. Center City, MN: Hazelden Publishing, 2010.

Browne, Sir Thomas. *Religio Medici*. New York: Collier, 1909.

Burns, David D. *Feeling Good: The New Mood Therapy*. New York: Harper, 2008.

Cameron, Julia. *The Artist's Way: A Spiritual Path to Higher Creativity.*
    10th anniversary ed. New York: Jeremy P. Tarcher/Putnam, 2002.

Casey, Karen. *Daily Meditations for Practicing the Course.* Center City,
    MN: Hazelden Publishing, 1995.

————. *Worthy of Love: Meditations on Loving Ourselves and Others.*
    Center City, MN: Hazelden Publishing, 1985.

Castillo, Stephanie. "Fighting Depression—Naturally: 6 Science-
    Backed Solutions." *Prevention,* May 7, 2013.

Chodron, Pema. *Good Medicine: How to Turn Pain into Compassion
    with Tonglen Meditation.* Sounds True CD AE00504, 2001,
    2 compact discs.

————. *When Things Fall Apart: Heart Advice for Difficult Times.*
    20th anniversary ed. Boulder CO: Shambhala, 2016.

Chopra, Deepak. *Peace Is the Way.* New York: Harmony Books, 2005.

Choquette, Sonia. *The Answer Is Simple . . . Love Yourself, Live Your
    Spirit!* Carlsbad, CA: Hay House, 2008.

Collins, Sonya. "In the No." *WebMD.* January 8, 2013. http://www
    .sonyacollins.net/2013 /01/08/in-the-no.

Covey, Stephen. *The 7 Habits of Highly Effective People: Powerful
    Lessons in Personal Change.* Revised ed. New York: Free Press, 2004.

Craig, Gary. *The EFT Manual.* Fulton, CA: Energy Psychology
    Press, 2011.

Davis, Laura. *The Courage to Heal: A Guide for Women Survivors
    of Child Sexual Abuse.* 20th anniversary ed. New York: William
    Morrow Paperbacks, 2008.

Dayton, Tian. *Trauma and Addiction: Ending the Trauma of Pain
    Through Emotional Literacy.* Deerfield Beach, FL: Health
    Communications, Inc., 2000.

DeMent, Iris. "No Time To Cry" on *My Life,* Warner Brothers CD
    9-45493-2, 1994, compact disc.

Dispenza, Joe. *Evolve Your Brain: The Science of Changing Your Mind.*
    Deerfield Beach, FL: Health Communications, Inc., 2008.

Dyer, Wayne. *Living an Inspired Life: Your Ultimate Calling.* Carlsbad,
    CA: Hay House, 2016.

————. *Wishes Fulfilled: Mastering the Art of Manifesting*. Carlsbad, CA: Hay House, 2013.

Emmons, Robert A. *Thanks! How Practicing Gratitude Can Make You Happier*. New York: Mariner Books, 2008.

Engle, Deb. *The Only Little Prayer You Need: The Shortest Route to a Life of Joy, Abundance, and Peace of Mind*. Newburyport, MA: Hampton Roads Publishing, 2014.

Feinstein, David. *The Promise of Energy Psychology: Revolutionary Tools for Dramatic Personal Change*. New York: Jeremy P. Tarcher/Penguin, 2005.

Feldman, Joan. *A Frog in My Basement: A Therapist's Curious Journey into Energy Psychology and the Law of Attraction*. Bloomington, IN: AuthorHouse, 2009.

Fox, Emmet. "The Golden Key." In *Power Through Constructive Thinking*. New York: HarperCollins, 1968.

————. *The Sermon on the Mount: The Key to Success in Life*. New York: HarperOne, 2009.

Fredrickson, Barbara, Michael Cohn, Kimberly Coffey, Jolynn Pek, and Sandra Finkel. "Open Hearts Build Lives: Positive Emotions, Induced Through Loving-Kindness Meditation, Build Consequential Personal Resources." *Journal of Personality and Social Psychology* 95, no. 5 (November 2008): 1045–62.

Gallo, Fred, and Harry Vincenzi. *Energy Tapping: How to Rapidly Eliminate Anxiety, Depression, Cravings, and More Using Energy Psychology*, 2nd ed. Oakland, CA: New Harbinger Publications, 2008.

Goyal, Madhav. "Meditation for anxiety, depression?" *ScienceDaily*, January 6, 2014. https://www.sciencedaily.com/releases/2014/01/140106190050.htm.

Heifetz, Ronald, and Marty Linsky. *Leadership on the Line: Staying Alive through the Dangers of Leading*. Boston: Harvard Business School Press, 2002.

Hill, Napoleon. *Think and Grow Rich*. Reproduction of the first edition, originally printed in 1937. Sound Wisdom: Shippensburg, PA, 2016.

Holzel, B. K., J. Carmody, M. Vangel, C. Congleton, S. M. Yerramsetti, T. Gard, and S. W. Lazar. "Mindfulness practice leads to increases in regional brain gray matter density." *Psychiatry Research: Neuro-imaging* 191, no. 1 (January 2011): 36–43. http://www.ncbi.nlm.nih .gov/pubmed/21071182.

Jampolsky, Gerald. *Love Is Letting Go of Fear,* 3rd ed. Berkeley, CA: Celestial Arts, 2010.

Jung, Carl. "Psychology and Religion." In *The Collected Works of C. G. Jung, Vol. 11, Psychology and Religion: West and East.* New Haven, CT: Yale University Press, 1938.

Kabat-Zinn, Jon. *Full Catastrophe Living (Revised Edition): Using the Wisdom of Your Body and Mind to Face Stress, Pain, and Illness.* New York: Bantam, 2013.

Kam, Katherine. "How Anger Can Hurt Your Heart." *WebMD.* April 27, 2015.

Katie, Byron. *Loving What Is: Four Questions That Can Change Your Life.* New York: Three Rivers Press, 2003.

Luskin, Fred. *Forgive for Good: A Proven Prescription for Health and Happiness.* New York: HarperOne, 2003.

Maletic, Vladimir, and Charles Raison. *The New Mind-Body Science of Depression.* New York: Norton, 2017.

Malloch, Theodore. *Being Generous.* West Conshohocken, PA: Templeton Press, 2009.

Murray, William Hutchinson. *The Scottish Himalayan Expedition.* London: J.M. Dent & Sons, 1951.

Neff, Kristin. *Self-Compassion: The Proven Power of Being Kind to Yourself.* Reprint ed. New York: William Morrow Paperbacks, 2015.

Paulson, J. Sig. *The Activity of God.* Lees Summit, MO: Unity Publications, 1969.

Peale, Norman V. *The Power of Positive Thinking.* Reprint ed. New York: Touchstone, 2003.

Remen, Rachel Naomi. *Kitchen Table Wisdom: Stories That Heal.* 10th anniversary ed. New York: Riverhead Books, 2006.

Rumi, Jalal al-Din. *The Essential Rumi, New Expanded Edition.* Reprint ed. New York: Harper, 2004.

Schucman, Helen, and Bill Thetford, eds. *A Course in Miracles.* Combined Volume. 3rd ed. Mill Valley, CA: The Foundation for Inner Peace, 2007.

Seligman, Martin. *Authentic Happiness: Using the New Positive Psychology to Realize Your Potential for Lasting Fulfillment.* New York: Free Press, 2002.

Shinn, Florence Scovel. *The Game of Life and How to Play It.* Reprint of 1941 Second Edition. Eastford, CT: Martino Publishing, 2011.

Sood, Amit. *The Mayo Clinic Guide to Stress-Free Living.* Philadelphia: Da Kapo Press, 2013.

Swami Amritaswarupananda Puri. *From Amma's Heart: Conversations with Sri Mata Amritanandamayi Devi.* Kerala, India: Amrita Books, 2010.

ten Boom, Corrie. *Clippings from My Notebook.* London: Worldwide Publications, 1982.

Tipping, Colin. *Radical Forgiveness: A Revolutionary Five-Stage Process to: Heal Relationships, Let Go of Anger and Blame, Find Peace in Any Situation.* Louisville, CO: Sounds True, 2010.

Tolle, Eckhardt. *A New Earth: Awakening to Your Life's Purpose.* New York: Penguin, 2008.

———. *The Power of Now: A Guide to Spiritual Enlightenment.* Novato, CA: New World Library, 1997.

Vitale, Joe, and Ihaleakala Hew Len. *Zero Limits: The Secret Hawaiian System for Wealth, Health, Peace, and More.* Hoboken, NJ: Wiley, 2007.

Vujicic, Nick. *Unstoppable: The Incredible Power of Faith in Action.* Colorado Springs, CO: WaterBrook Press, 2012.

Williamson, Marianne. *A Return to Love: Reflections on the Principles of "A Course in Miracles."* New York: HarperOne, 1996.

Woititz, Janet. *Adult Children of Alcoholics.* 2nd expanded ed. Deerfield Beach, FL: Health Communications, Inc., 1990.

Young, Wm. Paul. *The Shack: Where Tragedy Confronts Eternity.* Reissue ed. Newbury Park, CA: Windblown Media, 2016.

ABOUT THE AUTHOR

Gigi Langer holds a PhD in Psychological Studies in Education and an MA in Psychology, both from Stanford University. During her years at Eastern Michigan University, she won several awards for her teaching, and (as Georgea M. Langer) wrote four books for educators.

Gigi is a sought-after speaker who has helped thousands of people improve their lives at home and work. As a person in recovery, Gigi hasn't had a drug or drink for thirty years, although she does occasionally overindulge in Ghirardelli chocolate and historical novels. She lives happily in Michigan with her husband, Peter, and her cat, Murphy.